About this Book

Unlikely as it may seem, all domestic dogs are believed to be descended from a single ancestor, the wolf. This species was once the most widely distributed of all mammals in the Northern Hemisphere. The numbers of wolves in both Asia and North America have declined significantly. Within the remaining numbers there are still considerable differences in the physical appearance of wolves. The largest, the gray wolves, are found in Alaska, where they can weigh up to 177 lb, whereas those living in the steppes of the former Soviet Union are much smaller and lighter in color, averaging just 27 lb. This helps to explain why domestic dogs vary so widely in terms of size and coloration.

The domestication of the dog did not occur at one time or in one place, but in many places, starting more than 10,000 years ago, with probably four or five different races of the wolf contributing to the dog's ancestry. Today, there are about 400 recognizable breeds of domestic dog. In the United States, the American Kennel Club was founded in 1884 as the principal registry for dogs shown in America and people now marvel at the many breeds exhibited in regulated shows. Dog-owning and exhibiting has become a popular pastime for millions.

About half the world's breeds have now become well known internationally, but others remain rare and are popular only in limited areas. There has always been an interest in the exotic, but importing and establishing a new breed is a very expensive undertaking. The top 10 breeds in popularity in 1997 were the Labrador Retriever, Rottweiler, German Shepherd Dog, Golden Retriever, Beagle, Poodle, Cocker Spaniel, Dachshund, Pomeranian, and Yorkshire Terrier.

The world of dogs is a fascinating one, and whether you choose to have a single pet, or establish a kennel of show dogs, your life will be enriched significantly as a result.

To help you find the topics you require, there are three aids in the book: the contents, where all 300 questions are listed; the solution finders, which feature important questions with diagnostic charts showing the possible causes of symptoms and their likely solutions; and the index.

contents

3 DIET

8 BREEDING

9 BEHAVIOR

10 SHOWING

solution finder

I AM CONCERNED ABOUT MY DOG'S EATING HABITS.

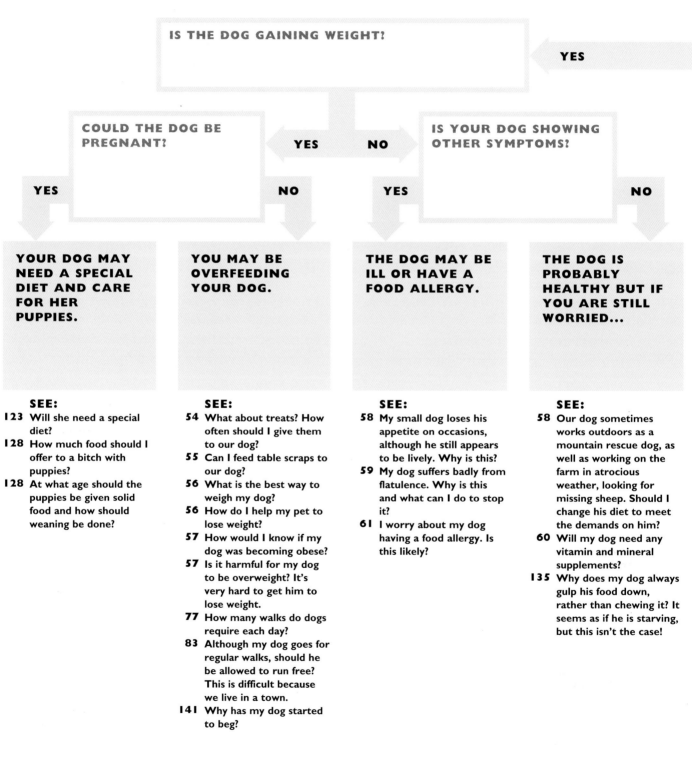

IS THE DOG GAINING WEIGHT?

YES

COULD THE DOG BE PREGNANT?

YES   **NO**

IS YOUR DOG SHOWING OTHER SYMPTOMS?

YES   **NO**   **YES**   **NO**

YOUR DOG MAY NEED A SPECIAL DIET AND CARE FOR HER PUPPIES.

YOU MAY BE OVERFEEDING YOUR DOG.

THE DOG MAY BE ILL OR HAVE A FOOD ALLERGY.

THE DOG IS PROBABLY HEALTHY BUT IF YOU ARE STILL WORRIED...

SEE:
- **123** Will she need a special diet?
- **128** How much food should I offer to a bitch with puppies?
- **128** At what age should the puppies be given solid food and how should weaning be done?

SEE:
- **54** What about treats? How often should I give them to our dog?
- **55** Can I feed table scraps to our dog?
- **56** What is the best way to weigh my dog?
- **56** How do I help my pet to lose weight?
- **57** How would I know if my dog was becoming obese?
- **57** Is it harmful for my dog to be overweight? It's very hard to get him to lose weight.
- **77** How many walks do dogs require each day?
- **83** Although my dog goes for regular walks, should he be allowed to run free? This is difficult because we live in a town.
- **141** Why has my dog started to beg?

SEE:
- **58** My small dog loses his appetite on occasions, although he still appears to be lively. Why is this?
- **59** My dog suffers badly from flatulence. Why is this and what can I do to stop it?
- **61** I worry about my dog having a food allergy. Is this likely?

SEE:
- **58** Our dog sometimes works outdoors as a mountain rescue dog, as well as working on the farm in atrocious weather, looking for missing sheep. Should I change his diet to meet the demands on him?
- **60** Will my dog need any vitamin and mineral supplements?
- **135** Why does my dog always gulp his food down, rather than chewing it? It seems as if he is starving, but this isn't the case!

IS THE DOG EATING AND DRINKING REGULARLY?

NO

IS THE DOG LOSING WEIGHT?

IS THE DOG EATING AND DRINKING OCCASIONALLY?

YES / **NO**

DOES THE DOG HAVE OTHER PROBLEMS?

YES / **NO** / **YES** / **NO**

THE DOG MAY HAVE PROBLEMS EATING OR IT MAY BE ILL.

THE DOG IS PROBABLY ILL.

THE DOG MAY BE EATING UNHEALTHILY OR THE WRONG FOOD.

YOUR DOG COULD BE EATING ELSEWHERE.

SEE:
49 How many meals a day does my puppy need? Should the number change as it grows older?
52 Do puppies need milk to drink?
52 If I use fresh food, how should I prepare it to ensure that our dog receives a balanced diet?
52 We're a vegetarian household. Can I feed our dog in the same way?
53 Is dry food better than canned food?
53 Can I feed my dog raw meat? Do dogs prefer cold food?
95 Should I brush my dog's teeth regularly? If so, what should I use?
100 How do I know if my dog is sick?

SEE:
40 How will I know when it is no longer fair to keep my dog?
59 My older dog has been diagnosed as suffering from chronic renal failure. Should I alter his diet?
59 Why does my dog eat grass? Is he missing something in his diet?
61 I worry about my dog having a food allergy. Is this likely?
103 Is there something wrong with my dog's diet? It seems to suffer regularly from episodes of diarrhea.
103 Why are female dogs more prone to urinary infections than males?
103 Are some breeds more prone to tumors than others?
104 How common are tumors in dogs, and what treatments are available?
104 My dog is very thin, and my veterinarian says that it could be suffering from pancreatic insufficiency. What is this?

SEE:
52 Do puppies need milk to drink?
52 If I use fresh food, how should I prepare it to ensure that our dog receives a balanced diet?
52 We're a vegetarian household. Can I feed our dog in the same way?
53 Is dry food better than canned food?
53 Can I feed my dog raw meat? Do dogs prefer cold food?
58 My small dog loses his appetite on occasions, although he still appears to be lively. Why is this?
61 I was disgusted when my dog ate its own feces. Why did it do this, and how can I stop it?
103 Is there something wrong with my dog's diet? It seems to suffer regularly from episodes of diarrhea.

SEE:
49 How many meals a day does my puppy need? Should the number change as it grows older?
49 How much should my dog drink?
51 Do dogs become bored eating the same food every day?
52 What type of food is best for my puppy?
146 Our dog keeps on stealing food. Why is this?

I AM WORRIED ABOUT MY DOG'S COAT

DOES THE DOG HAVE LESIONS OR SKIN IRRITATION?

YES

THIS COULD BE DUE TO DIET, PARASITES OR SKIN CANCER.

YES   **NO**

THE COAT CONDITION COULD BE A SIGN OF ILLNESS OR THE DOG IS OLD.

IS IT IN POOR CONDITION?

DO YOU GROOM YOUR DOG REGULARLY?

NO

YOUR DOG'S COAT SHOULD BE IN REASONABLE CONDITION AND SOME DOGS REQUIRE LESS GROOMING.

YES   NO

REGULAR GROOMING WILL PREVENT PROBLEMS, ESPECIALLY WITH LONGHAIRED DOGS.

SEE:

26 My son is asthmatic. Is it fair to get a puppy?
27 Is a dog that does not shed regularly a suitable choice as a pet for asthmatics?
27 What breed would be a good choice for a family pet with our children?
33 I'm worried about breed weaknesses associated with purebred dogs. What are the common problems?
85 How often is it necessary to groom our dog?
86 How much do grooming requirements vary according to individual breeds?
86 When should I start to groom my dog?

86 Do some dogs shed less than others?
88 How do I decide on the type of trim needed?
89 Should I have our dog groomed professionally?
90 How often should I bathe my dog?
91 What about actually washing my dog?

SEE:

85 How often is it necessary to groom our dog?
86 When should I start to groom my dog?
86 What should I do if my dog's coat becomes badly matted?
90 How often should I bathe my dog?
91 What about actually washing my dog?
92 What about drying my dog afterward—can I use a hair dryer?
92 How do I remove mud from my dog's coat and should I wash its feet after a walk?
93 Should I clean my dog's ears regularly?
93 My Pug suffers from tear-staining down its coat close to the eyes. Why is this and what can I do about it?
94 What tool is best to cut my dog's nails, and how should I carry out this task?
94 My dog still has its dewclaws. Please advise on clipping these back.
95 Should I brush my dog's teeth regularly? If so, what should I use?

I AM HAVING PROBLEMS WITH MY DOG'S ELIMINATION HABITS.

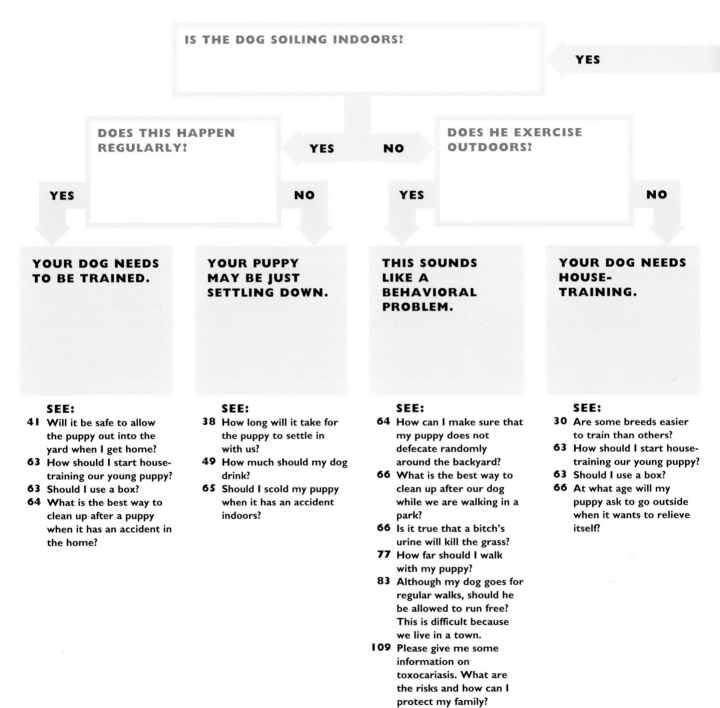

IS THE DOG SOILING INDOORS?

YES

DOES THIS HAPPEN REGULARLY?

YES **NO**

DOES HE EXERCISE OUTDOORS?

YES **NO** **YES** **NO**

YOUR DOG NEEDS TO BE TRAINED.

YOUR PUPPY MAY BE JUST SETTLING DOWN.

THIS SOUNDS LIKE A BEHAVIORAL PROBLEM.

YOUR DOG NEEDS HOUSE-TRAINING.

SEE:
41 Will it be safe to allow the puppy out into the yard when I get home?
63 How should I start house-training our young puppy?
63 Should I use a box?
64 What is the best way to clean up after a puppy when it has an accident in the home?

SEE:
38 How long will it take for the puppy to settle in with us?
49 How much should my dog drink?
65 Should I scold my puppy when it has an accident indoors?

SEE:
64 How can I make sure that my puppy does not defecate randomly around the backyard?
66 What is the best way to clean up after our dog while we are walking in a park?
66 Is it true that a bitch's urine will kill the grass?
77 How far should I walk with my puppy?
83 Although my dog goes for regular walks, should he be allowed to run free? This is difficult because we live in a town.
109 Please give me some information on toxocariasis. What are the risks and how can I protect my family?
109 What is the danger of children acquiring toxocariasis in public places?
141 Why does my dog scratch at the door to be let back into the house?

SEE:
30 Are some breeds easier to train than others?
63 How should I start house-training our young puppy?
63 Should I use a box?
66 At what age will my puppy ask to go outside when it wants to relieve itself?

IS IT A HOUSE-TRAINING PROBLEM?

NO

IS IT A URINARY PROBLEM?

COULD THE DOG BE ILL?   **YES**   **NO**   **IS IT A DEFECATION PROBLEM?**

YES   **NO**   **YES**   **NO**

HAVE THE DOG CHECKED BY A VETERINARIAN.

IT MAY BE A QUESTION OF TRAINING OR MODIFYING BEHAVIOR.

YOUR DOG MAY BE ILL. CHECK WITH YOUR VETERINARIAN.

IT MAY BE A BEHAVIORAL PROBLEM OR A MINOR HEALTH COMPLAINT.

SEE:
59 My older dog has been diagnosed as suffering from chronic renal failure. Should I alter his diet?
59 Why does my dog eat grass? Is he missing something in his diet?
61 I worry about my dog having a food allergy. Is this likely?
98 My dog is suffering from diarrhea, but appears lively. How long should I wait before contacting the veterinarian?
100 How do I know if my dog is sick?
103 Is there something wrong with my dog's diet? It seems to suffer regularly from episodes of diarrhea.
103 Why are female dogs more prone to urinary infections than males?

SEE:
64 How can I make sure that my puppy does not defecate randomly around the backyard?
66 Is it true that a bitch's urine will kill the grass?
142 What is the purpose of the anal sacs?

SEE:
98 My dog is suffering from diarrhea, but appears lively. How long should I wait before contacting the veterinarian?
103 Is there something wrong with my dog's diet? It seems to suffer regularly from episodes of diarrhea.

SEE:
59 My dog suffers badly from flatulence. Why is this and what can I do to stop it?
59 Why does my dog eat grass? Is he missing something in his diet?
109 Please give me some information on toxocariasis. What are the risks and how can I protect my family?
109 What is the danger of children acquiring toxocariasis in public places?
134 Why does my dog scratch at the ground after urinating?
140 Why do male dogs urinate over vertical objects, such as trees, while bitches and puppies of both sexes squat?

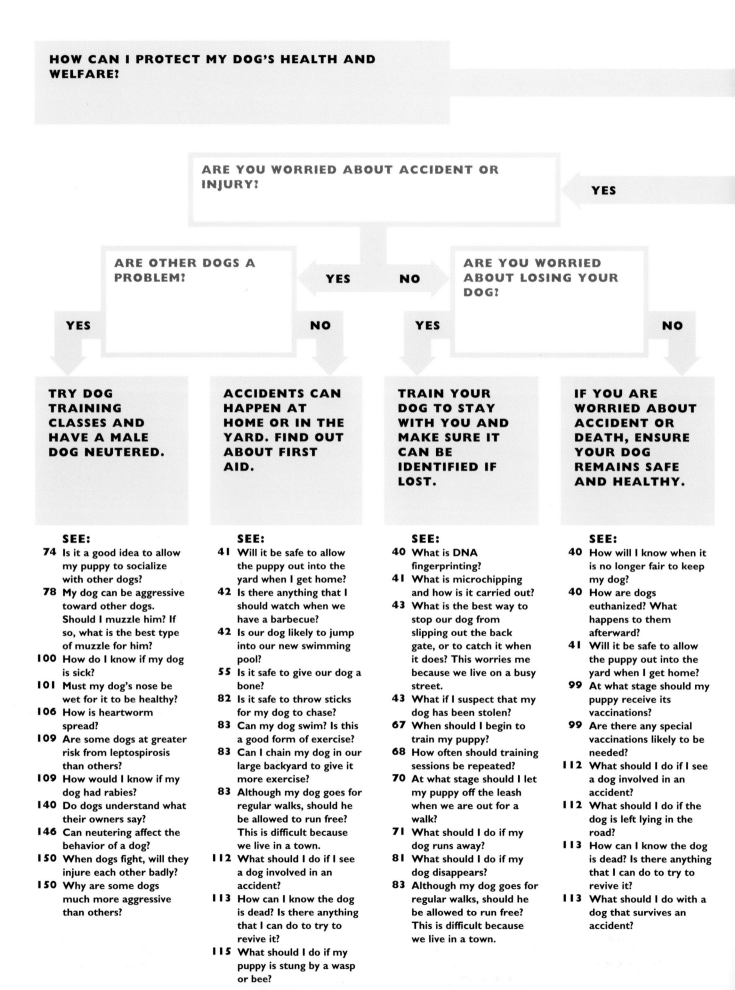

HOW CAN I PROTECT MY DOG'S HEALTH AND WELFARE?

ARE YOU WORRIED ABOUT ACCIDENT OR INJURY? — **YES**

ARE OTHER DOGS A PROBLEM? — **YES** / **NO** — **ARE YOU WORRIED ABOUT LOSING YOUR DOG?**

YES — **TRY DOG TRAINING CLASSES AND HAVE A MALE DOG NEUTERED.**

NO — **ACCIDENTS CAN HAPPEN AT HOME OR IN THE YARD. FIND OUT ABOUT FIRST AID.**

YES — **TRAIN YOUR DOG TO STAY WITH YOU AND MAKE SURE IT CAN BE IDENTIFIED IF LOST.**

NO — **IF YOU ARE WORRIED ABOUT ACCIDENT OR DEATH, ENSURE YOUR DOG REMAINS SAFE AND HEALTHY.**

SEE:
- 74 Is it a good idea to allow my puppy to socialize with other dogs?
- 78 My dog can be aggressive toward other dogs. Should I muzzle him? If so, what is the best type of muzzle for him?
- 100 How do I know if my dog is sick?
- 101 Must my dog's nose be wet for it to be healthy?
- 106 How is heartworm spread?
- 109 Are some dogs at greater risk from leptospirosis than others?
- 109 How would I know if my dog had rabies?
- 140 Do dogs understand what their owners say?
- 146 Can neutering affect the behavior of a dog?
- 150 When dogs fight, will they injure each other badly?
- 150 Why are some dogs much more aggressive than others?

SEE:
- 41 Will it be safe to allow the puppy out into the yard when I get home?
- 42 Is there anything that I should watch when we have a barbecue?
- 42 Is our dog likely to jump into our new swimming pool?
- 55 Is it safe to give our dog a bone?
- 82 Is it safe to throw sticks for my dog to chase?
- 83 Can my dog swim? Is this a good form of exercise?
- 83 Can I chain my dog in our large backyard to give it more exercise?
- 83 Although my dog goes for regular walks, should he be allowed to run free? This is difficult because we live in a town.
- 112 What should I do if I see a dog involved in an accident?
- 113 How can I know the dog is dead? Is there anything that I can do to try to revive it?
- 115 What should I do if my puppy is stung by a wasp or bee?

SEE:
- 40 What is DNA fingerprinting?
- 41 What is microchipping and how is it carried out?
- 43 What is the best way to stop our dog from slipping out the back gate, or to catch it when it does? This worries me because we live on a busy street.
- 43 What if I suspect that my dog has been stolen?
- 67 When should I begin to train my puppy?
- 68 How often should training sessions be repeated?
- 70 At what stage should I let my puppy off the leash when we are out for a walk?
- 71 What should I do if my dog runs away?
- 81 What should I do if my dog disappears?
- 83 Although my dog goes for regular walks, should he be allowed to run free? This is difficult because we live in a town.

SEE:
- 40 How will I know when it is no longer fair to keep my dog?
- 40 How are dogs euthanized? What happens to them afterward?
- 41 Will it be safe to allow the puppy out into the yard when I get home?
- 99 At what stage should my puppy receive its vaccinations?
- 99 Are there any special vaccinations likely to be needed?
- 112 What should I do if I see a dog involved in an accident?
- 112 What should I do if the dog is left lying in the road?
- 113 How can I know the dog is dead? Is there anything that I can do to try to revive it?
- 113 What should I do with a dog that survives an accident?

ARE YOU CONCERNED ABOUT YOUR DOG'S ENVIRONMENT?

NO

DO YOU WANT TO BREED OR SHOW YOUR DOG?

ARE YOU CONCERNED ABOUT PROBLEMS RELATING TO BREEDING AND SHOWING?

YES

NO

ARE YOU WORRIED ABOUT LEAVING YOUR DOG ALONE?

YES

NO

YES

NO

MAKE SURE THAT YOUR DOG IS VACCINATED AND BE AWARE OF POSSIBLE PROBLEMS.

BE AWARE OF WHAT TO EXPECT FOR YOU AND YOUR DOG.

PLAN AHEAD AND ENSURE THAT YOUR DOG WILL BE WELL LOOKED AFTER.

KEEP YOUR DOG HAPPY AND HEALTHY WITH A GOOD DIET, REGULAR HEALTH CHECKS AND GROOMING.

SEE:
89 Should I have our dog groomed professionally?
119 I want to breed from my bitch. How do I find a stud dog?
120 How do I prevent my bitch giving birth to a litter containing pups sired by two different male dogs?
121 What happens if the mating proves unsuccessful?
121 Is my dog at any risk of catching a sexually transmitted disease as the result of mating?
126 Are some breeds more prone to birth problems than others?
127 Will my bitch bond well with her puppies? Are there likely to be any problems in the immediate post-birth period?
127 What problems could arise during the weaning period?
129 Is it dangerous for bitches to breed late in life? Does their fertility decline?

SEE:
117 At what age do dogs become sexually mature?
117 What are the signs of sexual maturity?
118 How will I know when our bitch comes into heat?
118 Are male dogs only able to mate seasonally as well?
119 I want to breed from my bitch. How do I find a stud dog?
119 What arrangements should I make with the owner of the stud dog?
120 Should I have my bitch checked by my veterinarian before mating her?
122 How soon is my bitch likely to show obvious signs of pregnancy?
122 How do the unborn puppies develop?
123 Will she need a special diet?
123 Is it safe to exercise her normally during pregnancy?
153 How will I know if my puppy is a future champion?

SEE:
38 Will my puppy be as friendly if it lives in a kennel?
46 When we go on vacation, is it fair to take our dog with us?
46 What about booking our dog into a boarding kennel?
47 What are the usual procedures when using a kennel?
47 What if my dog gets sick while I am away?
47 Could someone look after my dog at home?

SEE:
52 What type of food is best for my puppy?
52 We're a vegetarian household. Can I feed our dog in the same way?
53 Is dry food better than canned food?
54 What about treats? How often should I give them to our dog?
57 Is it harmful for my dog to be overweight? It's very hard to get him to lose weight.
85 How often is it necessary to groom our dog?
90 At what age should my dog first be bathed?
93 Should I clean my dog's ears regularly?
93 My Pug suffers from tear-staining down its coat close to the eyes. Why is this and what can I do about it?
94 What tool is best to cut my dog's nails, and how should I carry out this task?
95 Should I brush my dog's teeth regularly? If so, what should I use?

I WANT TO UNDERSTAND AND, IF NECESSARY, MODIFY MY DOG'S BEHAVIOR.

IS YOUR DOG HOUSE-TRAINED → YES

YES

IS THE BEHAVIOR AGGRESSIVE OR FEARFUL?

YES   NO

NO → **DOES IT SOIL IN THE HOME?**

YES   NO

IT COULD BE TERRITORIAL BEHAVIOR, OR THE DOG COULD FEEL THREATENED.

THE PROBLEM COULD BE BEHAVIOR THAT NEEDS MODIFYING.

CHECK THAT IT IS NOT A MEDICAL PROBLEM.

IT IS A PRECAUTION TO HOUSE-TRAIN YOUR DOG.

IS THE BEHAVIOR ANTISOCIAL, OR DANGEROUS TO HUMANS OR OTHER ANIMALS?

NO

DOES THE BEHAVIOR OCCUR OUTDOORS?

THE BEHAVIOR MAY BE NORMAL FOR YOUR DOG.

YOUR DOG MAY BE ILL.

NO   **YES**

SEE:

117 What are the signs of sexual maturity?

118 How will I know when our bitch comes into heat?

132 Why does a dog curl in a ball at first when it sleeps and then stretch out?

135 Why does my dog always gulp his food down, rather than chewing it? It seems as if he is starving, but this isn't the case!

135 Why do puppies chase their tails?

136 Why do dogs roll on the ground?

139 Why is my bitch producing milk from her mammary glands, although she has no puppies?

141 Why has my dog started to beg?

141 Why does my dog scratch at the door to be let back into the house?

SEE:

39 If my dog plays outside during hot weather, will this make him more vulnerable to skin cancer?

59 Why does my dog eat grass? Is he missing something in his diet?

81 Is it really dangerous to exercise dogs when the weather is hot?

98 My dog is suffering from diarrhea, but appears lively. How long should I wait before contacting the veterinarian?

102 How do dogs pick up grass seeds?

102 Is there any other reason that may cause my dog to chew at its paw?

133 Why does my dog dig in the flower bed and try to bury its bone here?

134 Why does my dog scratch at the ground after urinating?

134 Why does my dog drag his hindquarters along the ground? Is this a sign of impending paralysis?

138 We live on a farm. Why does my Collie herd our livestock?

140 Why does my dog stop at every lamppost and lift his leg?

140 Why do male dogs urinate over vertical objects, such as trees, while bitches and puppies of both sexes squat?

There are many different aspects to choosing a pet, especially a dog that is likely to be part of your daily life for more than a decade. It is not something that should be rushed into without proper thought. It is much better to draw up a shortlist of different breeds than choose one just because you like its appearance. If you decide on a purebred, the costs involved, and the degree of care needed, will vary from breed to breed.

1 Choosing a Dog

Choosing a mixed breed dog can be very difficult for many people because of the huge variation in appearance of such dogs. The basis of the choice under these circumstances depends on looking at puppies or older dogs that are available at the time and finding a special dog with individual appeal.

your new dog

Choosing a suitable dog, and preparing your home for your canine friend.

HOW CAN I BE SURE THAT I CAN LOOK AFTER A DOG PROPERLY?

- You must be certain that you can meet a dog's needs, and make the necessary commitment to its well-being for a decade or more. It is important to look at your environment. Is there space for a dog? As a general rule, it is not a good idea to keep a dog in an apartment without access to a fenced yard. Your lifestyle also matters. If you live on your own, do you work long or irregular hours?

- Under these circumstances, you would probably be better off with another kind of pet. Dogs left alone for long periods are likely to become bored and destructive. They may also bark repeatedly and upset the neighbors.

- You will also need to consider the costs of feeding, veterinary care, and kennel fees.

- Assuming that these factors are not insurmountable, however, you can be certain that keeping a dog will be a great source of pleasure, in spite of the almost inevitable problems, such as scratched doors and soiled carpets.

- Everyone can have a dog if they are committed to exercise and care for it properly. Dogs have lived in cities for centuries; mosaics with the warning *cave canem* ('beware of the dog') have been found decorating the entrances of Roman homes over 2,000 years old. Companion breeds require little strenuous exercise and adapt to apartment dwelling with ease.

WE LIVE IN AN URBAN ENVIRONMENT. IS IT FAIR TO KEEP A DOG?

- Herding, hunting, coursing, and working breeds need a great deal of exercise and aren't usually as well suited to urban life.

- There is some increased risk of disease to urban dogs living in high-density populations, and it is important to keep your dog's vaccinations current.

AT WHAT AGE SHOULD I OBTAIN THE PUPPY?

- It is usual for a prospective owner to view a litter of puppies at around 5 weeks old, before they are ready to go to a new home. You can then make your choice, pay a deposit if requested, and pick up the puppy at around 8 weeks old. There is a key period in a dog's life, known as the socialization period, between 1–3 months of age, when it is exploring and learning about its environment.
- Puppies that have human contact and are handled, petted, and loved, bond quickly to their human handlers. They are less likely to be shy or withdrawn as they grow up. This is why it is better to obtain a puppy from a litter that has been reared in a home rather than a kennel. A puppy that is accustomed to handling will settle into its new environment and adapt more quickly than an older dog.

IS IT PREFERABLE TO OBTAIN A PUPPY AT A CERTAIN TIME OF YEAR?

- Try to avoid the period around Christmas, when your home is likely to be in a state of upheaval, because this will be disorienting for a young puppy, and you will probably not have the time to help it to settle in properly.
- Also, do not obtain a dog just before going on vacation, so that it will have to be returned to the kennel right away. This is especially important with a puppy, because it could seriously hamper its training.
- In an ideal world, the spring is probably the best time to start out with a puppy, because as the weather becomes warmer, the puppy can spend longer playing in the yard, and house-training in particular is likely to be easier through the summer months. The longer days ahead also mean that you will be able to spend more time playing with your puppy outdoors.

SHOULD I MAKE ANY CHANGES AROUND THE HOME IN ADVANCE?

- Be sure that your home and yard are free from toxic substances that can poison your puppy.
- Put all detergents, cleaners, automobile chemicals, insecticides, and fertilizers out of reach.
- Check your backyard fences for openings through which the puppy might escape.
- An indoor pen will confine the puppy when you can't be with it. Fit an infant gate on stairways to prevent the pup from climbing up the stairs or falling downstairs.

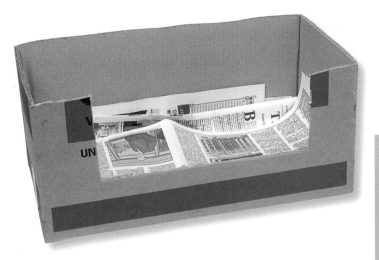

IS IT BETTER TO OBTAIN A DOG FROM A RESCUE ORGANIZATION THAN FROM A BREEDER?

- Breed rescue organizations are part of the breed club and specialize in the placement of purebred dogs.
- Rescue volunteers work closely with shelters to evaluate, train and re-home dogs of their breed. These dogs are residents of the rescue organization for many reasons. The history of a particular dog is often available from the organization. In order to make an intelligent decision regarding a pet, talk with the volunteers, and don't adopt a dog with a major behavioral problem, if it is known.
- Often older, stable dogs that are accustomed to children make better pets for a child than a puppy, but remember, the dog may be in the rescue organization because of a temperament problem. Take pets on a trial basis and if the dog doesn't fit into your family within two weeks, return it.

WHAT SHOULD I BUY FOR MY PUPPY BEFORE IT COMES HOME?

- The temptation is to rush out and purchase lots of equipment, but in reality you only need a few items at this stage.
- Food and water bowls (see page 50) are essential, and so is a collar of suitable size that can be let out as the puppy grows and its neck becomes thicker.
- Puppies have a chewing instinct; invest in some nylon bones and chew sticks. Since puppies of the larger breeds grow quickly, if you purchase a bed, be sure that it will accommodate an adult dog.
- If you have adopted a dog on trial, obtain a suitable cardboard box as a temporary bed, line the base with newspapers, and furnish it with an old blanket for bedding. Then, when needed, an appropriate bed can be purchased.

dogs & families

How to choose a dog to fit in with your lifestyle and that of your family.

- If your son is believed to be allergic to dog dander, try borrowing a dog from a friend for a few days. If the child shows no increased asthmatic signs, and if his or her doctor approves, you can proceed.
- If you purchase a puppy, consider keeping your son's bedroom door closed, to avoid his exposure to the dog during the night.
- Train the puppy to stay off the furniture, and vacuum daily to remove loose hair and dander from the environment.
- Groom the dog regularly outside, and choose a breed such as a Poodle that loses a minimum amount of hair on the furniture.
- Another good choice might be a Chinese Crested or Mexican Hairless; they are dogs with practically no hair, and their dander is quite easily controlled. You must consider the climate when choosing these dogs, since they don't adapt well to cold weather.

MY ELDERLY MOTHER WANTS A DOG. IS THIS A GOOD IDEA?

MY SON IS ASTHMATIC. IS IT FAIR TO GET A PUPPY?

- Recent studies have shown the benefits of pet ownership for people of all ages, especially the older members of society.
- Provided that your mother is relatively able-bodied, there is no reason why she should not have a dog.
- A dog provides great companionship and reassurance for someone living alone who spends much of his or her time at home. Burglars are usually far less likely to target a home where there is a dog, which should make your mother feel safer, especially at night.
- Try to persuade her to choose a small dog that she can control easily. A large, powerful dog might pull her over. An elderly person's lifestyle and physical capability are better suited to an adult dog than to a puppy. The grown pet is usually house trained, and needs less training, and less exercise than a young dog. If her yard isn't fenced, you might need a dog walker to help.

I'M NOT EAGER TO START OUT AGAIN TRAINING A PUPPY AT MY AGE. WILL AN OLDER DOG ADJUST WELL IN THE HOME?

- A carefully selected older dog will usually fit well into your home. You are less likely to have to clean up after it, or to have damage to your furnishings caused by its chewing.
- Don't take an older dog that has spent most of its previous life in a kennel. An adult dog that hasn't been house trained, and hasn't been taught to behave, is often harder to train than a puppy.
- If an older dog has been trained to walk on a leash, come when called, and is well-mannered in the yard or kitchen, it might prove to be a good prospect.
- Always take an adult dog into your home on trial, to be sure it will adapt to your lifestyle and you can adapt to its personality.

IS A DOG THAT DOES NOT SHED REGULARLY A SUITABLE CHOICE AS A PET FOR ASTHMATICS?

- All dogs shed their coats seasonally. While it is true that so-called hairless breeds have little hair, that which they have is shed seasonally.

- Allergies are often provoked by dander from a dog's skin glands, and hairless dogs also produce dander. To minimize the dander that is dropped from a hairless dog, wipe the dog down daily with a warm, wet cloth or a lotion.

- For a child's pet, avoid the toy or delicate miniature breeds that may be inadvertently injured by a youngster.

- The giant breeds are rarely good choices for the opposite reason; they grow quickly and may knock a small child over with their tail, or hurt the toddler when trying to play. Large dogs such as the Golden and Labrador Retrievers are usually tough, yet gentle, and therefore are popular children's pets.

- Smaller dogs that make excellent companions for children include the Cavalier King Charles Spaniel and the English Toy Spaniel. With any dog, remember to teach your children the proper ways to handle these pets. They must respect their companions as living beings that can't be treated as battery-operated toys.

WHAT BREED WOULD BE A GOOD CHOICE FOR A FAMILY PET WITH OUR CHILDREN?

HOW SHOULD I INTRODUCE THE PUPPY TO OUR CAT?

- It is best to allow them to meet and become acquainted on their own. If you try to introduce them directly, the puppy is likely to become upset and the cat may lash out with its claws, especially if it has not shared the home with a dog before.

- The puppy is likely to make the first advances, pursuing the cat for a short distance. A nervous cat may run off at this stage, while a more dominant feline will pause and stand its ground, which will probably cause the puppy to stop in its tracks. It may approach the cat more cautiously, and the cat might respond by cuffing the puppy if it ventures too close.

- Before long, the puppy will have learned its lesson, with the result that, in most households, the cat is the dominant individual. In cases where kittens and puppies are reared together, however, the bond between them is likely to be much stronger to the extent that they will even curl up and sleep together, and remain lifelong companions.

dog characteristics

Whether to get a mixed breed or a purebred, and deciding between a male and female.

- There is no reason why breeds that were developed primarily as guardians cannot be good household pets, particularly as they tend to be loyal and protective by nature toward people whom they know well. Dogs of Mastiff stock were originally bred to protect flocks of sheep and other farm stock from wolves.

- Problems are most likely to arise with such breeds today when they encounter strangers, particularly visitors to your home. Since most guard dogs are large, they are not the best choice for a home with young children. Early training is a must.

- The German Shepherd Dog has become one of the most popular breeds throughout the world, thanks not only to its alert nature, but also to its innate intelligence. Problems arise with some guard dogs when they are not properly trained, because they then revert to aggression to determine their social ranking, both with other dogs and with people.

- Children are most likely to be attacked under these circumstances, because they do not appreciate the warning signs.

CAN GUARD DOGS MAKE GOOD FAMILY PETS?

- This is one of the problems associated with mixed breeds.

- If both parents are known, you may predict that the pups will be about their size. If only one parent is known, and sometimes if both parents are known, the pups may mature to be large or small, depending on the genes inherited. Siblings of mixed breeding may vary tremendously in size. If the feet of a pup seem large for its legs, it will mature to a large dog.

- Males are usually larger than females. By 14 weeks of age, puppies will usually reach half their adult body weight. By 16 weeks, they should be two-thirds their adult height, and will assume much of their adult appearance. These are only rules of thumb.

HOW CAN I TELL HOW BIG A MIXED BREED PUPPY WILL GROW?

Guard dogs such as the Rottweiler (below) can make good family pets, but early training is essential.

Mixed-breed dogs can make interesting and appealing pets.

IS A MALE A BETTER PET THAN A FEMALE?

- You are unlikely to notice any great difference between the sexes before puberty. A male puppy, for example, will squat to urinate rather than lift its hind leg at this stage.
- Subsequently, however, you may find that male dogs are more combative than females, and they can display an increased tendency to leave their scent with their urine around the home and yard. This is how they establish their territorial claim to the area. Male dogs are also likely to stray if there is a female in heat in the neighborhood, and they may be reluctant to return under these circumstances.
- Females have two periods of heat annually, in most cases, during which they will need to be closely supervised to prevent an unwanted pregnancy. They can also suffer from false pregnancies (see page 139) that can lead to serious, although temporary, behavioral changes even in the case of a female that is normally very docile.
- Many people feel that females are somewhat more affectionate than male dogs, but this is a matter of personal opinion. The reproductive problems associated with both sexes can be dealt with by neutering, although this surgery is more costly in female dogs.

IS IT TRUE THAT MIXED BREED DOGS ARE BETTER AS PETS THAN PUREBRED DOGS?

- There are three kinds of dog: purebreds, out-crosses, and mixed breeds. Purebred dogs have parents of the same breed. They will mature to look more or less like their parents, and they will possess similar innate breed characteristics.
- Because a purebred will develop with certain fairly consistent characteristics, you can be more assured of what the dog will be like than you can with a mixed breed.
- When the parents are two different breeds that have similar genetic characteristics, their offspring might be called out-crosses. The mixed-breed, mongrel, or mutt is the result of the breeding of two mixed-breed dogs, or two dogs that are dissimilar in characteristics. These offspring may have the temperament or physical characteristics of either or neither parent. Their size, coat, color, and abilities are usually unpredictable.
- There is said to be an advantage to ownership of such a dog. They seem to possess heterosis, a hybrid vigor that helps protect them from genetic diseases, weaknesses, and malformations that may afflict purebreds. Usually these dogs make excellent pets, regardless of their parents, and most are interesting individuals.

purebred dogs

All you need to know about selecting the right breed, and which questions to ask.

DO THE BREEDS DIFFER GREATLY IN TEMPERAMENT?

- The temperament of dogs is hereditary to a great extent. Different purebreds have certain innate characteristics, but the temperament of dogs within any breed varies according to the male and female that are selected for breeding, and external factors, such as socialization and training, also have some bearing.
- When a breed is decided upon, analyze the temperament of both the pup's parents. If they are shy or grouchy, the pups are likely to express this characteristic. You can't be sure that a pup of an aggressive breed will be aggressive just because the breed has an aggressive reputation.
- Nor can you be sure that a pup will be friendly based on its breed characteristics. Ask questions about the breed, but place more credence in the attitude of the parents of your selection. When you have purchased a pup, treat it with respect, kindness, and love, and you will enhance its hereditary temperament.

ARE SOME BREEDS EASIER TO TRAIN THAN OTHERS?

- The breeds that have been developed to work closely with people represent the easiest training prospects. Sporting breeds can be recommended, as can herding dogs, although these types of dog often have activity levels that preclude urban living.
- Hounds are usually independent dogs, due to their instinctive trailing behavior, and are less responsive to companion dog training than others.
- Large, dominant breeds often require more training to control their territorial and inherent protective nature. Toy breeds often have minds of their own, and may resist even the most rudimentary training. Mixed breeds are often easily trained.

An elegant Dalmatian (below left), and an English Setter (below right) with typical feathering on its tail, legs and chest.

WHERE SHOULD I LOOK FOR A PUREBRED PUPPY?

- From a reputable breeder. Newspapers and dog magazine ads are a less desirable way to find puppies, since these ads may reflect "puppy mill" pups of questionable quality and health.
- Ask questions on the telephone about the dogs for sale, and only consider those that are registered, have pedigrees, and have parents that you can see and handle.
- Backyard breeders often are a source of companion pets, and you can't be sure of the animal's health or temperament. Pet stores may recommend reputable breeders in the area.

- If you obtain your new pet from a reputable source, you will minimize the likelihood of problems. Do not rush into a decision—allow yourself time to watch the puppies. You can then see that a puppy moves freely and looks alert. Check specific points.
- Ask the seller if you can pick up the puppy. The eyes should be clean, with no sign of discharge. The coat should also be clean, with no fleas, ticks (see page 105) or other parasites. Check

HOW CAN I MAKE SURE THAT MY PUPPY IS HEALTHY?

particularly at the rear end, as staining in this area could indicate diarrhea.

- A puppy's body is covered with pliable skin, and you may be able to feel the ribs, which is normal. Run your hand along the middle underside of the body to be sure there is no swelling, which would indicate an umbilical hernia, necessitating surgical correction.
- A potbellied appearance may be indicative of intestinal worms. Do not worry too much if the ears are not erect in a breed that should have erect ears. In the case of the German Shepherd, for example, it may take six months for the ears to assume their characteristic raised position.
- Check the legs to see if the dewclaws, which are usually removed when the puppy is just a few days old, are still present.
- Dewclaws, especially hind ones, may be easily snagged on carpet or brush, and if ignored, they may grow into a circle and penetrate the skin. If they are clipped regularly, they aren't likely to cause problems, but unless they are a breed feature, it is better to have them removed shortly after birth.

WHY DO PURE-BREDS VARY GREATLY IN PRICE?

The Wire Haired Pointing Griffon is a purebred hunting dog, but its good temperament makes it ideal for a family pet.

- Prices, for the most part, reflect the individual animal's conformation to the breed standard. Excellent examples of any breed will demand higher prices than average for "pet quality" dogs.
- There is usually an additional price level for dogs of rare breeds compared to those that are seen on the street every day. If the best puppy is selected from an excellent litter that was the result of a champion bred to a champion, the price is going to be high.
- If the breed is rare, it will be even higher. In working dogs, a similar pricing schedule is usually at play. If a pair of excellent purebred herding dogs is mated, and you pick the choice pup of the litter, you will pay for it. Companion dogs of all breeds are usually available at more reasonable prices because of slight conformational, coat, or color faults. It pays to call various breeders and inquire.

WHAT QUESTIONS SHOULD I ASK BEFORE DECIDING ON A PUPPY?

- Ask yourself whether you like the puppies available. Remember that the puppy is likely to be part of your daily life for over a decade, so it pays to be patient when starting out. You may want to discuss grooming requirements.
- In a number of breeds, such as Chihuahuas, there are both long-coated and short-coated versions—the latter generally needs less grooming.
- Bear in mind that longhaired puppies typically have less profuse coats than adults, although the pattern of their markings will remain consistent throughout their lives.
- Do not rush a purchase, but take your time. You may, for example, not like the puppy's markings. If you are not happy for any reason, do not feel obliged to take one of the puppies available, but look elsewhere.
- Having made your choice, find out about the puppy's dietary requirements. Ask what type of food it is eating, and how many meals, so that you can continue with this regimen at first. Avoid sudden changes, which are likely to cause a digestive disturbance. Find out what vaccinations the pup has received, and obtain its vaccination certificate. In the case of a purebred dog, you will also need its pedigree information so you can register the puppy in your name. The breeder should already have registered the litter with the American Kennel Club (AKC).

(right) Three Pembroke Welsh Corgi puppies at 8 weeks old.

HOW DO I FIND A REPUTABLE BREEDER?

- Reputable breeders can be found by attending dog shows and field trials. Their names can be obtained by contacting breed clubs listed by the American Kennel Club (AKC).
- Reputable breeders will have pedigrees of all their dogs, and you can easily ascertain the origin and quality of their puppies.
- They will have health papers and histories of all their pups, and will not allow a shopper to take a puppy that is not in perfect condition.
- They will insist on a veterinary examination of a purchased pup if that has not already been accomplished. They will provide you with a written guarantee that allows you to return a defective puppy within a certain period.
- Most important, they will question you about your reason for buying a pup and your ability to provide for one.

The Pekingese is a dignified and fearless dog but can have health problems due to its flattened face.

I'M WORRIED ABOUT BREED WEAKNESSES ASSOCIATED WITH PURE-BRED DOGS. WHAT ARE THE COMMON PROBLEMS?

● Hereditary problems are always a concern. Take your new puppy to a veterinarian for an examination and discuss with him or her all hereditary problems that are known in the breed. Ask about hip dysplasia, since this hereditary disease affects most giant, large, and many smaller breeds. It is the result of a weakness of the hip joints, in which the ball of the femur does not fit snugly into the socket joint on the hip above. In mild cases there may be few signs of the condition, but in severe cases lameness is common.

● Elbow dysplasia is a similar weakness affecting the elbow joint. Patellar luxation is another common hereditary fault, especially in toy breeds. The ligaments that should hold the patellas (or kneecaps) firmly in position are loose, so that there is no support for the lower leg. This affects general coordination and causes the dog to drag its legs. The signs usually become apparent when the dog is around five months old.

● Hereditary eye problems are frequent in many breeds, and your discussion should include progressive retinal atrophy, entropion, ectropion, and cataracts. Some breeds have a predisposition to epilepsy, and others tend to develop hypothyroidism. Bone diseases, such as osteochondritis dessicans, should be discussed, as well as many others. Many of these hereditary diseases develop later in life. They are treatable, but few can be prevented.

● Ask the breeder if there have been any genetic disorders in the pup's bloodline, and if its parents have been certified free of any defects commonly afflicting the breed.

HOW WILL I KNOW WHICH PUPPY IN THE LITTER IS LIKELY TO MAKE THE BEST PET?

● The most practical way is to observe the pups from a distance for a while. See if one is more aggressive than the others, plays more, chews on its mother, barks, and tackles its siblings.

● Note pups that hide and seem shy of people. Slowly approach the litter and kneel down to their level.

● Find a puppy that is curious, but not aggressive. Don't take the shy pup, because it probably needs the comfort of its mother for another week. Pick a puppy that isn't afraid when you play with it.

● Then stand and walk away, and look over your shoulder to see which pups are following you. Kneel down and pick one of them up and take it into another room. Play with it one-on-one for a few minutes.

● If its tongue is licking everything in sight and its tail is wagging furiously, you have made a good choice for a companion.

Observe the pups from a distance and find one that is lively and curious, but not aggressive.

Dogs are creatures of routine and this is an important
consideration when caring for them. If you leave your dog alone for
long periods, you are likely to find that it has been destructive. Try
to anticipate your dog's needs in advance so that the likelihood of

2 General Care

problems will be minimized at the outset. It is also important to
involve other members of the household in the dog's care, so that
your pet will respond positively to them in your absence. It will
usually take longer to accustom an older dog to a new routine,
compared with a puppy, but with patience, even an older individual
will settle in well. Dogs that have been kept in doghouses or
kennels for years will find it difficult to adapt to a domestic life
indoors.

young puppy

How to accustom your new puppy to your home, and care for all its needs.

WHEN SHOULD I GIVE THE PUPPY ITS FIRST MEAL?

- Feed the puppy the same quantity and brand of food that was being fed by the breeder. Feed it at about the times of its previous feedings.
- Don't change its feeding schedule in any way for a week.
- Don't be alarmed if the pup doesn't eat immediately after arriving in your home. After it has explored the house and yard, offer it fresh water and food. If it again refuses to eat, wait until after it has taken a nap, and when awake, it will probably eat. If it doesn't, pick the food up after five minutes and try it again in a couple of hours.
- If you find that the pup is eating less than the breeder indicated, feed it less. It is important to feed only the amount that the pup will eat in a few minutes.

HOW SHOULD I PICK UP A PUPPY?

- Support the pup on your hand and arm so it is comfortable, and use your other hand to cover its body to steady it. Be sure to support the entire body.
- Watch out for the puppy's claws, which are very sharp at this stage. Pick up the puppy while you are sitting on the floor at first. After it has adjusted to your handling, stand slowly to avoid frightening it.
- Give the pup a feeling of security and don't let it slip or drop. Never pick up a puppy by the skin of its neck, or with one hand. This is the primary bonding time for your pet, and it is important to let the pup realize that you are to be trusted.
- After rising from the floor, walk about slowly until the pup becomes adjusted to your body movement.
- Then slowly place it back on the floor, being sure that all four of its feet are on the ground.

● Try to pick a place where the bed can remain indefinitely. Choose a quiet location, where noises and activities are minimal. Since pups often have their eliminations following naps, pick a spot than can be easily cleaned and lay down newspaper for the puppy to "go" on. A utility room or a room with a tile floor is best. If you have such a room near the back door, it will be more convenient for house-training. If you have purchased a carrying kennel or indoor pen for the dog, this is the time to use it. Place the bed in the kennel or pen.

WHERE SHOULD I PUT MY PUPPY'S BED?

● The pup will no doubt cry and whine to be allowed more freedom, but the best service you can perform is to ignore the noise, unless you are beginning house training. In that case, respond to its howling by taking it outside. It is usually not a good idea to allow the puppy to sleep in any location that won't be its permanent place.

● If you take the puppy into your bed on the first night, resolve to allow it to occupy that space when it is full-grown.

WHERE CAN I OBTAIN A KENNEL FOR MY DOG?

● Check the advertisements in dog magazines and visit pet supply companies, fence companies, and lumber suppliers.

● You should be able to find either ready-made housing for your dog, or the materials with which to construct a doghouse.

● In shopping for doghouses, look at the insulation, the flooring, and the size of the house.

● Don't forget that your pup will grow up and require more floor space than it does now.

● It is important that the kennel is easy to clean, and has an impermeable floor to keep the pup dry. It needs to be waterproof and solidly built.

- Heating a kennel with electricity can be extremely dangerous. Don't try it yourself.
- Remember that dogs can chew through cables and into heating elements, especially during storms and other frightening events.
- If you wish to provide heat in the dog's kennel, consult with a professional builder who has done similar work before. It's better to provide a warm place for your dog in your home in foul weather.

I WANT TO HOUSE OUR PUPPY IN AN OUTDOOR KENNEL. WILL THIS BE ALL RIGHT?

- Outside kennel use depends on the pup's previous habitat, the breed, the season of the year, and your facilities.
- A pup must be given shelter from the elements, warmth, and security. If these are present in your outside kennel, it is suitable.
- A run in the proximity of the kennel is vitally important.

- Designs are available from lumber suppliers and from libraries in case you decide to build the kennel yourself. Choose lumber that is not preserved with chemicals that are harmful to the dog, because puppies chew. Slope the run from front to back to establish drainage, and raise the floor of the doghouse from the soil by setting it on a layer of bricks.
- Set the posts of the run in concrete so that they will stand the wind and weather for many years. Choose fencing that will withstand chewing and weathering; the best is chain-link fencing.

HOW SHOULD I CONSTRUCT THE KENNEL AND RUN?

WILL MY PUPPY BE AS FRIENDLY IF IT LIVES IN A KENNEL?

- Puppies are friendly by nature, but they do need to be with humans as much as possible.
- If you keep your pup in a kennel at night, let it out into a fenced yard during the day. Never use confinement in the kennel as a punishment.
- Keep in mind that if a dog is confined to an outdoor kennel it will never be house-trained.

A puppy should be kept in a kennel for security and confinement only at night.

- A pup is usually bought as a companion, and it is difficult for it to fill that role while living outdoors in a kennel.
- In most situations, the kennel should be used for security and confinement only at night.

HOW LONG WILL IT TAKE FOR THE PUPPY TO SETTLE IN WITH US?

- The time it takes for a pup to adjust to a new situation depends on its age and how it is handled. If you are consistent in your treatment of a 7–10-week-old pup and keep it on a regular schedule, it will adapt to your home and lifestyle within a week.
- If you play with the pup, and train, pet, and groom it every day, it will quickly become a member of the family.
- Use coaxing and some small tidbits to teach it the name you have chosen to call it by.
- Reward it for coming to you when called, and for asking to go outdoors.
- Be kind and considerate to the pup and it will reciprocate.

Handling the puppy will help it settle in with the family.

adult dog

General health concerns with older dogs, and the importance of regular checks.

HOW SHOULD I PICK UP A LARGER, OLDER DOG?

- This depends on the size of the dog being lifted. In any case, reassure the dog.
- Kneel down beside it and speak in low, soothing tones as you gradually place your arms around the dog.
- One of your arms should encompass the dog's hind legs, just under its rump, with the other arm around the forelegs, just under its neck.
- Hold its body close to you and lock your hands together in the region of the dog's rib cage, keeping its head away from your face.
- Then slowly, gradually stand.
- If the dog is of a size that can be supported with one hand and steadied with the other, place one hand and arm beneath its breastbone, tucking its hindquarters against your body, and the other in front of its neck.
- Always move slowly and be sure the dog feels secure in your arms.

ARE ROUTINE HEALTH CHECKS A GOOD IDEA FOR MY ELDERLY DOG?

- Routine health examinations for older dogs are invaluable.
- A trained veterinarian will discover conditions that might escape your notice, and early treatment can be initiated.
- Your dog will live a longer, happier life because of these annual or semiannual checkups.

- The ambient temperature has nothing to do with skin cancer. Sunshine can precipitate skin cancer if the dog is predisposed to that disease.
- A dog with white ears, eyes, or muzzle, or a pink nose rubber is more apt to get skin cancer than one with darker pigmentation. Sunburn in dogs has similar effects to those that occur in humans; it can lead to many serious problems.
- If your dog's skin is relatively unpigmented, especially in the region of its head, be sure it always has shade from the sun.
- Consult with your veterinarian to obtain advice about preventive treatment.

IF MY DOG PLAYS OUTSIDE DURING HOT WEATHER, WILL THIS MAKE HIM MORE VULNERABLE TO SKIN CANCER?

HOW WILL I KNOW WHEN IT IS NO LONGER FAIR TO KEEP MY DOG?

- Considering euthanasia can be very difficult.
- Discuss your feelings and your dog's condition with your veterinarian.
- Think very carefully about your dog's quality of life.

- Can it move about without pain?
- Is it able to eat and drink comfortably?
- Does it show interest in walks?
- If any or all of these questions receive a negative response, and there is no hope of the dog's recovery, it may be time to say good-bye to your companion.

WHAT IS DNA FINGERPRINTING?

- DNA (deoxyribonucleic acid) is the genetic material that is present in the nucleus of every living cell in the body. It contains the unique hereditary code of each individual. DNA can therefore be used to identify a particular dog, and to indicate whether or not a puppy was bred from its stated parents (provided that the relevant samples are available for comparison). DNA is not yet used routinely for recognition purposes, but it may become a factor in particular situations, such as identifying a dog that has been attacking sheep. For more information on DNA testing, contact the United Kennel Club (UKC): (616) 343-9020.

- Talking about her feelings is important.
- Ask your veterinarian to put you in touch with a trained bereavement counselor, who is familiar with the sense of loss and other emotions that can be stirred up by the death of a loved pet.
- The situation is likely to be especially painful if your mother owned the dog before she was widowed, because the dog represented a link to your father.
- Your mother may not want another dog of her own at this stage, but you may be able to persuade her to act as a foster-carer for homeless dogs.
- Temporary homes are frequently needed while such dogs await new owners. This is likely to bring your mother into contact with a new group of people, and she may even decide to become involved in other aspects of the group's work.

MY WIDOWED MOTHER IS DISTRAUGHT AT THE LOSS OF OUR DOG. HOW CAN I HELP HER COME TO TERMS WITH HER GRIEF?

HOW ARE DOGS EUTHANIZED? WHAT HAPPENS TO THEM AFTERWARD?

- The usual method is to inject a barbiturate into a leg vein.
- It is identical to the procedure used to administer an injectable anesthetic, except that a lethal dose is given.
- The dog loses consciousness almost immediately, with no signs of distress, and its heart ceases to beat very shortly afterward. Your veterinarian can dispose of the dog's body for you, or you can have it returned to you for burial.

- Many owners choose a plot in a pet cemetery, where they can visit their dog's grave.
- Some owners choose cremation.

safety first

How to ensure that your new dog is safe in the home, and easily identified if lost.

ARE THERE LIKELY TO BE ANY PROBLEMS MOVING TO OUR NEW HOUSE WITH OUR DOG?

- Dogs generally adapt well to a move, but some precautions are needed. Consider placing your dog in a kennel or having it cared for during the move to avoid the possibility of its slipping through an open door during the upheaval, or causing an accident by getting underfoot.
- Check the fences and gates of your new home carefully. If there was a dog in the house before, change the carpets to remove all traces of the previous pet.
- Otherwise your dog may urinate around the house to exert its dominance and mask the scent of its predecessor.

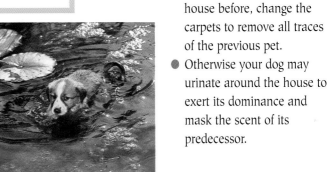

WILL IT BE SAFE TO ALLOW THE PUPPY OUT INTO THE YARD WHEN I GET HOME?

- While it is not advisable to allow a young, unvaccinated puppy into public places, such as parks, your backyard should be safe enough.
- There are some diseases that can be spread by foxes, raccoons, coyotes, and other wild animals if they should stray into your yard. If you suspect this is happening, you need to ensure that they cannot get into the yard.
- Physical hazards are a more serious concern, and you should be mindful of swimming pools, ponds, and other pets that may gain access to your yard (see page 42). It is usually safe to allow your dog to run freely within a fenced yard anytime you are there.
- Giving the pup free admittance to a yard will let you begin house-training right away.

- This is a permanent way of identifying a dog by means of a microchip placed just under the skin. It is becoming increasingly popular. The tiny microchip unit is inserted through a syringe-like dispenser in a virtually painless procedure. Once in place, the unit remains inert, but its unique code can be revealed by passing a scanner over the area of the implant. There are more than three billion possible codes, so there is no risk of duplication. The dog's number can be recorded at a central registry, so that if your pet subsequently strays and loses its name disk it can be readily traced. Contact the American Kennel Club (AKC) for information on microchipping your dog: 1-800-252-7894.

WHAT IS MICROCHIPPING, AND HOW IS IT CARRIED OUT?

IS OUR DOG LIKELY TO JUMP INTO OUR NEW SWIMMING POOL?

IS THERE ANYTHING THAT I SHOULD WATCH WHEN WE HAVE A BARBECUE?

- All breeds of dogs can swim, but that doesn't address the dangers of pools. When the pool is filled with people, the dog will very likely join them, muddy feet and all.
- When no one is in the yard, the dog may decide to go for a swim, and won't be able to get out of the pool unless there are steps provided that it can handle.
- Empty pools are especially hazardous to dogs that may not realize the depth of the hole into which they might jump.
- If your pool doesn't have a dog-proof security fence, make sure the pup is confined in its run or in the house when not on a leash.

- It depends upon the number of guests and their understanding of the puppy's strict dietary restrictions. If you think that the pup is likely to snatch some food from a guest's plate, or from the grill, it's best to shut the puppy in its run or confine it to the house.
- If the group is small and trustworthy, let them enjoy the antics of the pup.
- Be sure that all food scraps are placed in containers that are out of reach of the puppy when the barbecue is over.
- Remember that sauces and condiment spills will be inviting to the pup, and they are likely to cause an upset stomach.
- Don't allow anyone to feed the dog from his or her plate.

WHAT IF I SUSPECT THAT MY DOG HAS BEEN STOLEN?

● Report your loss immediately to the police, along with any relevant information, such as suspicious calls or visitors.

● Dog theft is a particular risk for rare breeds or top show winners, whose value is high. Identification by microchip or tattoo will prevent disputes over ownership.

● In other cases, you may have to rely on markings, evident in photographs of your pet, or scars, warts, and other identifying features confirmed from veterinary records. It is possible to insure dogs against theft.

● This may be an additional feature of an insurance policy, but check the fine print carefully, especially if you have a valuable dog.

WHAT IS THE BEST WAY TO STOP OUR DOG FROM SLIPPING OUT THE BACK GATE, OR TO CATCH IT WHEN IT DOES? THIS WORRIES ME BECAUSE WE LIVE ON A BUSY STREET.

● If your dog wanders out undetected, it will probably amble up the street, sniffing at scents along the way.

● A greater danger will occur if you see the dog heading off and shout at it, because it may then respond by dashing away across the street.

● Place particular emphasis on teaching your dog to stay when instructed, and always remain calm and still while calling your dog back to you.

● The safest option for small dogs is to fix a secondary barrier on the inner side of the gate. Although you will need to step over this, it will prevent your dog from escaping.

traveling

How to make traveling a comfortable experience for your dog.

WHAT IS THE BEST WAY TO TRAVEL WITH A PUPPY?

- A hard-sided carrier is a must if you travel often with your dog. It will confine the dog safely.
- Be sure that the carrier you purchase is large enough to house your dog as an adult.
- Other options for the confinement of dogs in automobiles are wire mesh pens, but they are a lot of trouble.

- If you use one for a young puppy, you must place layers of newspaper under the pen to absorb urine. In any case, a blanket and an old sweater or other article of clothing that belongs to the owner should be placed in the carrier. The scent of the owner will help calm the pup during the trip.
- If you travel with your adult dog and you don't choose to put it in a carrier, use a net or barrier to separate the dog from the front seat, so that it does not distract the driver.

- This is a possibility, especially since puppies are not used to the sensations of travel. If you are taking your pup home for the first time, it is also likely to be distressed at the separation from its littermates, and whining could exacerbate the problem.
- If your puppy vomits, stop the car and replace the bedding at the earliest opportunity, so that its coat doesn't become soiled.
- To overcome motion sickness, take your puppy out

IS THE PUPPY LIKELY TO BE CAR SICK?

regularly for short drives, and it should grow out of the tendency. It is a good idea, in any case, to accustom dogs to travel from an early age, so they will not be nervous about car journeys in later life. If traveling continues to upset your dog, consult with your veterinarian and ask him or her to provide suitable medication to calm it when necessary.
- There are also herbal products available for this purpose.

HOW CAN I KEEP MY DOG COMFORTABLE IN THE CAR ON A HOT DAY?

- Heatstroke is a major problem with dogs left in cars.
- Every year during the warm months, dogs die needlessly because their owners leave them in cars that become quickly overheated.
- Never leave your dog alone in a car for more than five minutes in the summertime.
- Be sure the windows are open a few inches, and provide fresh drinking water for the dog.
- Even with these precautions, dogs have suffered heatstrokes in unattended cars.

WE HAVE TO FLY TO OUR NEW HOME WITH OUR DOG. HOW CAN THIS BE ORGANIZED?

- Airlines are generally very efficient at handling live animals in transit.
- Speak with the airline that you intend to fly with, so that they can tell you the necessary requirements.
- There is no live animal inspection at the airports, but when flying abroad, you must be prepared to deal with the health regulations of the country into which you are traveling.
- In the United States, interstate travel by common carrier requires a written health certificate from a veterinarian.
- Advice relative to taking your dog interstate or into another country is available from your veterinarian, or from travel agents specializing in dog-related trips.

vacations

Making provision for your dog's care when you are away on vacation.

WHAT ABOUT BOOKING OUR DOG INTO A BOARDING KENNEL?

- Try to obtain recommendations for local kennels, based on the experience of other dog owners, or possibly your veterinarian, and arrange to view the premises.
- This will give you the opportunity to see the facilities and to meet the staff. It is essential that the surroundings are clean and well-maintained, and that the staff should appear genuinely interested in the dogs and aware of their needs.
- If you are happy with the kennel, make your reservation well ahead of time, because kennels frequently become full at peak vacation periods.

WHEN WE GO ON VACATION, IS IT FAIR TO TAKE OUR DOG WITH US?

- This depends upon your destination. It is not practical to take your dog abroad by air for a vacation. If you plan a driving vacation, however, you could travel with your dog.
- Check your route carefully to include overnight stops at hotels that allow pets into rooms.
- Obtain this information from special guidebooks that cover the topic, or from the hotels.
- Give your dog the opportunity to exercise regularly each day during your vacation, so that it will not be restless on the journey, and be sure to have sufficient drinking water and food available.
- Never leave your dog alone in the car (see page 45).

MY DOG IS GOING INTO A BOARDING KENNEL FOR THE FIRST TIME AND I'M WORRIED ABOUT KENNEL COUGH. WHAT CAN I DO?

- Vaccination for kennel cough can offer protection, but it is not a positive assurance that the dog won't be infected. The vaccine may be reliable in some regions and not in others due to the difference in secondary bacterial infections that prevail. The infection may not be serious in otherwise healthy individuals, but may lead to pneumonia in aged or stressed dogs.
- It is spread by airborne droplets in the cough of an infected dog, and it may take five to ten days for signs to appear.
- The illness is usually identified by the onset of a harsh, dry cough, which occurs when the laryngeal area is touched.
- The cough may last for three to six weeks, but the course of the disease may be shortened by antibiotic therapy.

COULD SOMEONE LOOK AFTER MY DOG AT HOME?

- You will probably be asked to pay a deposit when you make a reservation, and to settle the remaining amount when you bring your dog to the kennel. This is because some unscrupulous owners abandon their pets at kennels.
- Lessen the stress on both of you by booking your dog into the kennel a day before the upheaval of your departure.
- Be sure that all the dog's vaccinations are current, and take the vaccination certificate to the kennel.
- You may want your dog to receive an additional vaccination against kennel cough (see left).
- It is usually unnecessary to provide food for your dog, unless it requires a special diet.
- A familiar toy or blanket may help your pet to settle down in its temporary surroundings.

WHAT ARE THE USUAL PROCEDURES WHEN USING A KENNEL?

WHAT IF MY DOG GETS SICK WHILE I AM AWAY?

- If your dog is suffering from any condition for which it is already receiving medication, make this clear to the kennel right away.
- They may not be able to take your pet under these circumstances. If your dog is an intact female, and she is likely to come into season, the kennel may refuse her.
- A female in heat can cause severe disruption in a kennel, with all the male dogs trying to reach her.
- Assuming that there are no obvious health problems with your dog, however, simply give the kennel a note of the name, address, and telephone number of your veterinarian, for use in case of an emergency, with your contact details.

- House-and pet-sitting services are becoming increasingly popular, partly as a way of lessening the risk of burglary in the homeowner's absence. If you plan to use such a service, check references and bonding, and talk to the people who will be caring for your dog. The service can be useful for an old dog, who might find it difficult to adapt to a kennel, or for a sick individual for whom the kennel is not an option. Although more costly than kenneling for one dog, pet-sitting can be an economical alternative if you have a number of pets. Be sure that the terms are clearly stipulated in advance, in writing, and notify your insurance company that your home will be occupied by someone else while you are away.

Feeding dogs is very straightforward and even if you are a vegetarian, your dog can enjoy a balanced diet that will keep it in good health. When feeding your dog, be sure to follow the recommendations on the package describing the amount of food that your dog will require. If a dog

3 Diet

is not exercised adequately, it will inevitably start to become obese before long. Regular monitoring of a dog's weight is therefore very important.

food facts

Practical facts about how much food to give your dog, how often, and tips on serving and storage.

HOW MANY MEALS A DAY DOES MY PUPPY NEED? SHOULD THE NUMBER CHANGE AS IT GROWS OLDER?

- From weaning to about 3 months of age, a puppy should be fed three times daily.
- From 3 months, twice a day feeding is sufficient. At a year of age, most adult dogs can be fed once daily, but prefer to receive two meals.
- As the dog matures, the amount fed per day is increased gradually to keep the dog in good condition. Free-choice feeding is another alternative, especially in adult dogs. Don't feed your adult dog after strenuous exercise, or before playing with it.
- Exercise following a meal may predispose the larger breeds to gastric torsion, a life-threatening condition that requires immediate veterinary attention.

HOW MUCH SHOULD MY DOG DRINK?

- This depends upon a variety of factors, including the dog's diet and its environmental temperature.
- Dogs that eat dry foods require more water to drink than those fed on canned food which has a higher moisture content.
- During hot weather, dogs are likely to drink more frequently to help keep themselves cool.
- A female that is suckling puppies needs additional fluid because of the water lost in her milk. Always provide a supply of fresh drinking water, and remember to take water if you are going out for the day. A water container that doubles as a drinking bowl can be useful under these circumstances.
- It is important to monitor your dog's fluid consumption, since excessive thirst can be a sign of certain health problems, including kidney failure and diabetes insipidus. If you notice that your dog has started to drink far more than normal, seek advice from your veterinarian.

WHAT TYPE OF FOOD BOWLS ARE BEST?

- Solid stainless steel bowls are preferable to any other kind.
- Earthenware bowls are sometimes porous and collect microscopic food particles that make them nearly impossible to clean.
- Plastic bowls can be chewed and their porosity is a problem as well.
- Choose a type of bowl that isn't easily tipped over by the dog, or buy a rack that holds the bowl upright.
- Long-eared dogs are best fed in bowls with small openings at the top to keep their ears from trailing in their food and water.

IS IT SAFE TO PUT THEM IN THE DISHWASHER?

- Stainless steel bowls are dishwasher-safe but they should be precleaned separately to prevent dog food residues from getting on your dishes. Washing and disinfecting dog dishes by hand in hot water and detergent is usually sufficient.
- If you disinfect the dog's bowls, use a disinfectant recommended especially for this purpose, in accordance with the manufacturer's instructions. Suitable products can be found in most pet stores.
- Rinse the dishes thoroughly, and dry them completely with paper towels before refilling, especially if you are using dry food, which absorbs moisture readily.

DO DOGS BECOME BORED EATING THE SAME FOOD EVERY DAY?

- We have no reason to believe that boredom with food plays any part in a dog's appetite.
- Many dogs that are fed the same dry dog food for years are happy and active. Some foods are more palatable than others and naturally they will be preferred.
- When you add meat scraps to a nutritionally balanced dry food diet occasionally, the dog may refuse to eat its normal diet for a day or two thereafter. This is the dog's way of telling you it prefers the taste of the scraps. The dog doesn't know that the scraps do not contain balanced nutrition.
- The key is to find a dog food that is palatable and nutritious and stay with it.

Dog food comes in a variety of forms. You will need to try out different types of food to see which suits your dog best.

- Store dry dog food in a moisture-proof dark container to minimize loss of nutrients and to prevent them from attracting rodents, roaches, and crickets.
- Keep this container at room temperature, because high summer temperatures also have a detrimental effect on the food.
- Use the food before the expiration date that is printed on the sack. If feeding semi-moist food, keep the packages in the cupboard, fold the top of a partially used pack, and finish it as rapidly as possible.
- They don't require refrigeration, but will dry out quickly after opening. Once a can has been opened, keep the remaining food in the refrigerator with a plastic lid firmly in place to prevent the food from drying out and to keep the smell of the dog food from permeating the fridge.
- Use the contents of the can as soon as possible.

HOW SHOULD I STORE MY DOG'S FOOD?

which food?

Outlines the food choices for your dog to ensure it receives balanced nutrition.

- Bitch's milk is significantly different from the milk of other species of animals. When a dam weans her brood, their need for milk ceases. Feeding milk, either raw or pasteurized, regardless of the fat content, will often cause diarrhea in the pup.
- Milk replacers are available in pet supply stores, and are used for orphaned puppies before weaning time. They need not be fed past six weeks of age.
- Milk products such as cottage cheese may be mixed in small quantities with puppy foods that are complete and balanced.

DO PUPPIES NEED MILK TO DRINK?

- There is no single best food. The nutritional content and the balance of these nutrients are critically important to your puppy. Prepared dog foods are divided into three basic categories. Canned food, which contains about 80 percent water, looks like meat, but may be formulated with practically no meat content. Dry dog food contains 10 percent water or less, and is more economical than canned food. Semimoist food is the third type and is sold in packets. It also has the appearance of meat, but may be formulated without a meat element. It often contains sugars and preservatives that are questionable sources of nutrition.
- Dry food is sometimes mixed with canned to increase palatability. This practice is fine, as long as both canned and dry foods are balanced nutritionally. The label information is critical. Use only dog food that supplies needed nutritional elements for the age and category of the dog being fed. Dogs that are in a rapid growth phase, in training, working, or raising puppies require a different food from that of adult companion dogs.

WHAT TYPE OF FOOD IS BEST FOR MY PUPPY?

- Getting a dog to eat a vegetarian diet is possible, but it's not easily accomplished.
- To formulate such a diet in your kitchen will require a course in canine nutrition, especially when you consider the difference in quantities of certain nutrients that are needed for growth, reproduction, work, and heavy activity.
- A dog's nutritional requirements are not the same as that of a human.
- The dog is a carnivore; we are omnivores. There are some dry food diets on the pet supply shelves that are vegetarian, and if you can find one of these that is complete and balanced, you could try it.

WE'RE A VEGETARIAN HOUSEHOLD. CAN I FEED OUR DOG IN THE SAME WAY?

IF I USE FRESH FOOD, HOW SHOULD I PREPARE IT TO ENSURE THAT OUR DOG RECEIVES A BALANCED DIET?

- A dog fed entirely on fresh food runs a much greater risk of nutritional deficiency than one whose diet consists of specially formulated dog foods. For example, the calcium to phosphorus ratio in organ meat will be inadequate, because the major store of calcium is in bone; Vitamin A, which is stored essentially in the liver, is likely to be lacking in other body tissues.
- Trying to compensate by mixing a dry food with meat upsets the balance that is built into the dog food.
- Dog food manufacturers, university researchers, and various foundations have now discovered exactly how much of each nutritional element is necessary and advisable in your pet's diet.
- If in doubt about feeding fresh food to your dog, consult with your veterinarian.

- Dog food manufacturers have invested huge amounts in researching the dog's nutritional requirements and putting them into palatable products. Both of these foods will therefore meet your dog's nutritional needs.

IS DRY FOOD BETTER THAN CANNED FOOD?

- Dry food is more convenient to use, but some dogs, especially the smaller toy breeds, find it less appealing than canned food.
- Loss of interest in dry food by an older dog may indicate a dental or kidney problem and should be reported to your veterinarian.
- At this stage in a dog's life, it may be necessary to switch to a specially formulated diet.
- One benefit of dry food is that it results in more compact stools for easier cleanup.

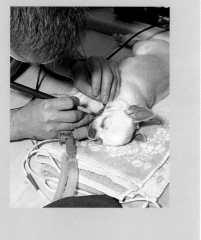

- We have a choice when we buy dog foods. Antioxidants are necessary additives that are used to preserve the quality and freshness of the foods. Certain antioxidants must be listed on the dog food label. Other foods are formulated with natural antioxidants, such as Vitamins E, A, and C.

I'M WORRIED BY ADDITIVES IN DOG FOOD— HOW SAFE ARE THEY?

- They are usually more expensive to use than the chemical preservatives, thus the dog food costs more. The choice is yours: read the label on the dog food; write or call the manufacturer and ask what preservatives are used; then make your selection.

- A dog's nutritional needs change at different stages of its life, and you must adapt its diet accordingly.
- Begin feeding your puppy a regular young dog's diet by the time it is about six months old, when the puppyhood stage ends.
- Always introduce changes gradually, mixing new food with your dog's regular diet over several days. Obviously you will need to increase the amounts to reflect the dog's growth.
- Life-stage diets that are formulated to meet the requirements of different-aged dogs can be a useful choice.

SHOULD I CHANGE A PUPPY'S DIET AS IT GETS OLDER?

CAN I FEED MY DOG RAW MEAT? DO THEY PREFER COLD FOOD?

- Feeding a dog on raw meat, cooked meat, eggs, or other food mixtures that you might formulate in your kitchen is not recommended.
- Rarely are these homemade diets complete and nutritionally balanced.
- The occasional use of small amounts of cooked meat that are added to the dog's regular balanced diet may not hurt the dog unless it interferes with its appetite.
- Excessive meat protein is not necessarily good for a dog, and will often cause dietary deficiencies. Tiny pieces of cooked meat may be used as bait when training a dog. Any dog food is best fed at room temperature.
- Heating dry dog food by adding a small amount of hot water makes it more palatable, and when feeding refrigerated food, always heat it to room temperature.

dog treats

Keep your dog healthy by sensible feeding with just an occasional treat.

WHY IS IT DANGEROUS FOR DOGS TO EAT OUR CHOCOLATE AND YET THEY CAN EAT DOG CHOCOLATE?

● Chocolate contains a chemical, theobromine, which stimulates the dog's central nervous system.

● An excessive intake of this can be fatal to a dog. Your dog will not appreciate the danger, so it is essential to place chocolates well out of your pet's reach.

● The chocolate produced for dogs, as drops or in treats such as cookies, does not contain theobromine, and is therefore safe. It does, however, contain calories, and its sugar content means that it cannot be recommended for dogs, except very occasionally.

WHAT ABOUT TREATS—HOW OFTEN SHOULD I GIVE THEM TO OUR DOG?

● There is an ever-growing array of dog treats on the market.

● Choose carefully and don't be too generous with them, because overindulgence could cause your dog to become obese. Treats add nothing to a balanced diet.

● They may be useful rewards during training, but don't use them every time, or you will lead your dog to always expect this kind of encouragement.

● There are better alternatives in any case, such as a small piece of carrot, which most dogs will eat happily.

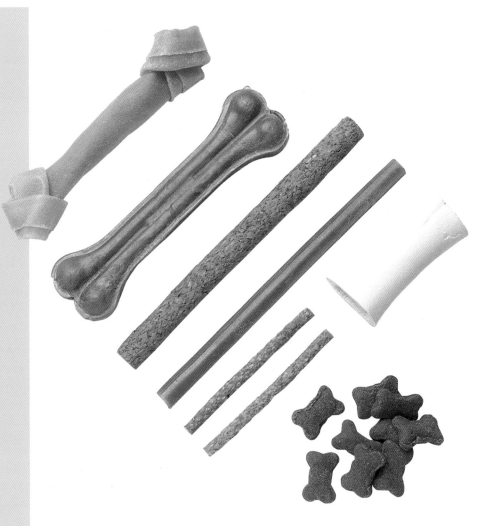

- In many cases, dogs instinctively prefer a bone to a chew, but if they are provided with chews from an early age, they take to them readily.
- Chews are especially valuable during the teething period, when the dog may otherwise seek to relieve the irritation in its mouth by gnawing at other objects around the home.
- Chews range from savory delights, such as dried pig ears and rawhide, to those made from artificial materials. They are avilable in shapes and sizes to appeal to dogs of all types. Dogs have individual preferences, so provide a selection to discover which kind of chew your pet likes best.
- As with a bone, it is essential to train your puppy to drop the chew on command, because otherwise, it will be reluctant to do so when it is older, and may bite if you try to take the chew away.

DO DOGS PREFER CHEWS TO BONES?

IS IT SAFE TO GIVE OUR DOG A BONE?

- Many dogs enjoy gnawing on bones and this can help to prevent the accumulation of tartar deposits on the teeth. It is important only to provide large marrow bones for your dog, however, because smaller bones can stick in the dog's throat and cause it to choke if swallowed. Chicken and rabbit bones are particularly dangerous, because they splinter easily.
- Do not allow bones on carpets or leave them lying around in hot weather, creating a hygiene risk.

CAN I FEED TABLE SCRAPS TO OUR DOG?

- It is not a good idea to do this routinely, because it unbalances your dog's regular diet, and could lead to obesity.
- The dog may also start to misbehave during your meals in anticipation of receiving food. If you do feed leftovers sometimes, avoid too many vegetables, which are likely to cause flatulence.
- Check that there are no bones, which could become lodged in your dog's throat; avoid fish in particular for this reason. Dogs will usually refuse spicy food, and feeding them the fatty remains of meat is obviously undesirable.

weight watching

Discusses the action to take if your dog starts to become overweight.

WHAT IS THE BEST WAY TO WEIGH MY DOG?

- This depends partly on the size of your dog.
- A small breed can stand on a bathroom scale to be weighed.

- In the case of a larger dog, however, the best solution is to climb on the scale yourself with your pet in your arms, being sure to keep both of you directly above the scale. Note your combined weight, and then subtract your weight from the figure to determine the weight of your dog.
- In the case of a purebred, some breed standards give you a clear indication of what is considered to be the ideal weight, but in the case of mongrels and crossbreeds, this can be more difficult.
- You may be able to gain an approximate idea from comparing the dog's weight with that of a purebred dog of similar size and stature, but consult with your veterinarian for precise information.

HOW DO I HELP MY PET LOSE WEIGHT?

- Obesity can occur gradually, so that by the time it is clearly apparent, fairly drastic action may be required.
- You can obtain an obesity diet from a pet supply store or from your veterinarian. This has a high fiber content to satisfy the dog's appetite but is relatively low in calories.
- Cutting back on food is not enough, however, because obesity is usually also a reflection of lack of exercise. You may need to take your dog for longer walks, or encourage it to become more active by throwing a ball or Frisbee that it can chase and return to you. In this way, the dog will cover nearly twice as much ground as you, and will use more energy as a result.
- Discuss the reducing program with your veterinarian, and monitor your dog's progress on a regular basis. Always weigh your dog in the morning, before providing a meal, to obtain a consistent figure, and keep a chart of its weight loss.

HOW WOULD I KNOW IF MY DOG WAS BECOMING OBESE?

- One of the most obvious signs would be that you could no longer feel your dog's ribs. You may also notice a reluctance on the part of your pet to exercise as vigorously as in the past, and possibly more panting following exertion of any kind, while its appetite remains unchanged.
- Obesity is becoming a serious problem in domestic dogs. Studies show that approximately 30 percent of the canine population in many countries is overweight.

Panting following exertion of any kind can be a sign of an obese dog.

- Obesity can shorten a dog's life considerably and must be treated. Contrary to widespread belief, spaying or neutering does not cause obesity. Weight gain usually occurs after sexual maturity, when spaying is done, and the surgery may then be blamed for the condition. Obesity can be associated with metabolic diseases, such as diabetes, but is more often the result of the dog consuming more calories than it burns.
- In the average family, the dog eats only what it is fed. If your dog is obese, cut back on its caloric intake and stop all snacks. Plan an exercise program and stick to it.
- Always take your dog to a veterinarian for a physical examination before a reducing program is begun.
- It may take time, but the reward will be a more active, lively companion.

IS IT HARMFUL FOR MY DOG TO BE OVERWEIGHT? IT'S VERY HARD TO GET HIM TO LOSE WEIGHT.

Increase your dog's exercise and reduce its caloric intake to help it to lose weight.

special needs

Dietary concerns, special diets for allergies, and energy-giving foods.

MY SMALL DOG LOSES HIS APPETITE ON OCCASIONS, ALTHOUGH HE STILL APPEARS TO BE LIVELY. WHY IS THIS?

- Small breeds are likely to be fussier about their food than their larger relatives are. If you change your dog's diet, and especially its consistency, your dog is unlikely to eat with its former enthusiasm.
- Dental problems can also be to blame. Some small dogs do not lose their deciduous (puppy) teeth, and if these are still present with the emerging permanent teeth, they could be a source of pain.
- In older dogs, kidney failure can have a detrimental effect on appetite.
- Take your dog to the veterinarian for a physical examination to exclude the possibility of a health problem.
- Environmental conditions may be a factor. Loud noises, such as thunder or fireworks, can cause a small dog to lose interest in food, as can the presence of strangers in your home.
- If there is a female dog in heat in the neighborhood, your dog may be more intent on getting out than on eating his meals.

OUR DOG SOMETIMES WORKS OUTDOORS AS A MOUNTAIN RESCUE DOG, AS WELL AS WORKING ON THE FARM IN ATROCIOUS WEATHER, LOOKING FOR MISSING SHEEP. SHOULD I CHANGE HIS DIET TO MEET THE DEMANDS ON HIM?

- There are diets formulated to provide greater energy for dogs with active lifestyles, and it sounds as if your dog could benefit from one of these.
- An alternative could be to increase the amount of meal in his diet. This would provide an additional source of carbohydrate, which is broken down in the body to supply energy.
- Such diets should be used only for active dogs, however, because otherwise the excess carbohydrate will be converted into fat.

The Bernese Mountain Dog makes an affectionate and loyal pet.

- Chronic renal failure affects all older dogs to some extent. There is no cure for the condition, but it can be stabilized, at least temporarily. Increased thirst and a correspondingly higher urinary output are the classic symptoms.

MY OLDER DOG HAS BEEN DIAGNOSED AS SUFFERING FROM CHRONIC RENAL FAILURE. SHOULD I ALTER HIS DIET?

- This is because the dog's kidneys can no longer concentrate the urine effectively. More water is lost through them, and a greater volume must be drunk in order to maintain the body's fluid balance.
- A nephritis diet, prescribed by your veterinarian, can help to alleviate the symptoms.
- The diet is formulated to lower the dog's overall protein intake while including protein of high biological value, such as that derived from eggs, to meet the dog's nutritional requirements.
- It is vital to provide your dog with a plentiful supply of water at all times, because dehydration is a constant risk of this condition, and can prove fatal.

WHY DOES MY DOG EAT GRASS? IS HE MISSING SOMETHING IN HIS DIET?

- Some people believe that dogs eat grass to compensate for a lack of fiber in their regular food.
- Dogs are choosy about the kind of grass they eat, and prefer tough, woody stems to short lawn grass.
- There is little nutritional value to be gained from this type of grass, especially since dogs lack the necessary enzymes to break down the cellulose in grass and digest it properly.
- A dog may consume grass as an emetic, and such behavior could be an attempt to rid itself of roundworms by vomiting.
- If you suspect worms, take a sample of the dog's stool to your veterinarian to check microscopically for worm eggs.

- This problem may be due to vegetables in the dog's diet, which affect its intestinal tract, or to food scavenged away from home.
- It is not always easy to overcome, but a probiotic that includes yucca extract may help. Another remedy is garlic, obtainable in capsules formulated for dogs from pet supply or health food stores.
- Charcoal-based cookies may not appeal to your dog but can be beneficial.

MY DOG SUFFERS BADLY FROM FLATULENCE. WHY IS THIS AND WHAT CAN I DO TO STOP IT?

WHAT ABOUT PROBIOTIC PRODUCTS? SHOULD I USE ANY OF THESE?

- Studies showed that dogs recovering from intestinal surgery benefit from the addition of live natural yogurt to their diet in the post-operative period, because of the presence of Lactobacillus bacteria.
- Subsequently it became apparent that while antibiotics can upset the protective bacterial population in the gut, probiotics, such as those present in yogurt, stabilize the beneficial gut flora, and help to protect the dog against harmful microbes, including salmonella, which can cause severe diarrhea.
- Probiotics are valuable for dogs that have been subjected to stress, from a change of environment, for example.
- A newly acquired puppy could benefit from such a product. Similarly, when a young dog has suffered from diarrhea, a probiotic can help to protect its intestinal tract from additional infections, and thus assist recovery. It is more effective to add the probiotic to your dog's food than to give it in drinking water.

WILL MY DOG NEED ANY VITAMIN AND MINERAL SUPPLEMENTS?

- A properly formulated diet will normally provide your dog with all its nutritional requirements.
- Pregnant bitches and young puppies, especially the larger breeds, may need a calcium supplement.
- Older dogs whose kidneys are failing can benefit from a vitamin B supplement, because these vitamins are likely to be lost in the urine.
- Such a deficiency may be indicated by a blackish tip to the older dog's tongue.
- Consult your veterinarian before giving your dog any supplements.

IS IT TRUE THAT SOME DOGS MAY SUFFER FROM SCURVY?

- It is estimated that roughly one in a thousand dogs is unable to manufacture this vital vitamin in its body, and it will then be vulnerable to a deficiency if vitamin C is not present in its diet.
- Signs of scurvy in dogs are not dissimilar to those seen in people, with cracking of the skin and subsequent bleeding being quite typical. Once this condition has been diagnosed, you will need to continue supplementing your dog's diet for the rest of his life. This can be carried out most simply by using vitamin C tablets, which are quite inexpensive, and they can be concealed in the dog's food, or given directly. It is generally recommended to give 1 g of vitamin C per 55 lb. body weight.
- Unfortunately, ascorbic acid, the active ingredient of this vitamin, has a short shelf life, so do not purchase more tablets than you are likely to require, based on the expiration date, and be sure to store them in a dark place, as this vitamin is adversely affected by sunlight.

Supplements are often supplied in the form of a palatable powder that can be sprinkled over the dog's food.

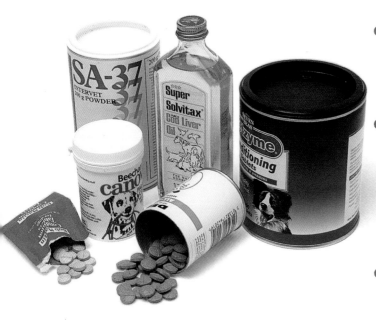

- This activity tends to occur in dogs that have been in kennels for long periods of their lives, especially if that environment did not conform to scrupulous standards of hygiene.
- It is different from the case of a dam with young puppies, for whom it is normal behavior to consume the stools of her offspring as a means of helping to conceal their presence.
- Discuss the problem with your veterinarian who can give you substances to add to the dog's food. These will make the dog feel ill if it attempts to eat its feces.
- Another underlying cause of this behavior can be a deficiency of certain important B vitamins. These are manufactured by beneficial bacteria in the dog's large intestine but cannot be absorbed from there. It may therefore be helpful to supplement the dog's diet with brewer's yeast tablets or powder, which are rich in B vitamins.

I WAS DISGUSTED WHEN MY DOG ATE ITS OWN FECES. WHY DID IT DO THIS, AND HOW CAN I STOP IT?

WHAT TYPE OF SUPPLEMENT SHOULD I USE?

- General-purpose supplements that contain a range of water-soluble vitamins, fat-soluble vitamins, minerals, and trace elements are most often used.
- Water-soluble vitamins are eliminated from the body, and therefore need to be replaced regularly. Fat-soluble vitamins are stored in the liver, and excessive doses can be harmful. Trace elements are inorganic substances that are required in minute amounts and play a key role in the metabolic process.
- The supplements are often supplied in the form of a palatable powder that can be sprinkled over the dog's food and will not deter it from eating.
- Liquid supplements are formulated to be mixed with water. Adding these to your dog's drinking water can be unreliable, because you can't be sure how much the dog will drink.
- A better method may be to dilute the supplement in water, and use the solution to soak dry food, so that your dog absorbs the supplement along with its food.
- Some specific supplements, such as brewers' yeast, come in tablet form, and are tasty enough for dogs to enjoy eating as they are. Follow the label recommendations rigorously when using any supplement, to avoid the risk of overdose.

I WORRY ABOUT MY DOG HAVING A FOOD ALLERGY. IS THIS LIKELY?

- A food allergy manifests itself in the form of itchy, sensitive skin, and often a rash. Some dogs appear to be vulnerable to this type of problem.
- It can be difficult, to determine whether a dog's symptoms are due to food intolerance, because there are numerous other possible causes, including infestation with fleas or other parasites, and allergies to bedding.
- If these have been eliminated and a food allergy is suspected, it is necessary to discover which food is the culprit. The usual approach is to feed the dog a plain diet, such as chicken and rice, and to add other ingredients one by one over a period of time to try and determine which food provokes an adverse reaction. This can be a time-consuming process. An alternative, provided all other possible causes of allergy have been eliminated, is to use a hypoallergenic diet.

A well-trained dog is a pleasure to own, but a troublesome individual will be a constant source of worry and concern. Fortunately, today it is easier than ever before to obtain advice and assistance regarding any difficulties with the training process. Although it is harder to train a mature dog than a

4 Training

puppy, this should not be regarded as an impossible task. Consistency and an even-tempered response on the part of the trainer are the secrets of success. Encouragement always works better than repeated scolding, which can cause a dog to lose confidence. If your dog seems to have difficulty understanding what is expected of it, give it clear commands to avoid confusion.

house-training

Training your pup to be clean around the home, and how to clean up after it.

- Puppies are instinctively clean by nature and will soon adopt a routine if they are clearly shown how to behave at an early stage.
- The keys to success are anticipation and positive encouragement.
- Place the young dog outdoors first thing in the morning, and last thing at night, when it is likely to want to relieve itself.
- Give the puppy an opportunity to go outside after each meal, since eating triggers the digestive process. Use a command that the puppy will come to recognize and associate with this activity, such as "Clean dog!"
- Always praise the puppy when it responds positively. In the initial stages, it is a good idea to go outside and stay with your puppy, so that it doesn't wander off around the backyard.

HOW SHOULD I START HOUSE-TRAINING OUR YOUNG PUPPY?

SHOULD I USE A BOX?

- This can be helpful if you need to leave your puppy indoors for longer than usual, but don't provide it on a regular basis, because the puppy may prefer to use the box instead of going outdoors.
- Choose a simple box that gives the puppy easy access to the interior; a hooded box, such as those sometimes used by cats, is likely to be ignored.
- Place some sheets of newspaper under the box, in case of accidents, and line it with newspaper so that you can lift out the entire contents and wrap them neatly for disposal.

OUR PUPPY SEEMS TO HAVE NO BLADDER CONTROL—IS IT REALLY LIKELY AT THIS STAGE?

- Puppies urinate frequently, but you need to distinguish between normal urination and a developmental problem affecting the urinary tract.
- Under normal circumstances, urine flows from each kidney down the ureters to the bladder, where it is stored. When the bladder fills to a certain point, the puppy releases the urine from the body through the urethra.
- Normal urination occurs in a regular flow, whereas incontinence can usually be identified by the presence of a relatively constant dribble of urine.
- This is generally caused by the weakness of the muscle sphincter that controls the flow of urine from the bladder. Consult with your veterinarian if you suspect such a problem.

- Buy a carpet disinfectant that is formulated to break down enzymes in urine and remove the scent of it. Many household disinfectants, especially pine-based products, reinforce the odor. As a result, the puppy will be attracted back to the spot and will urinate there repeatedly. Before you use the product on your carpet, check that it will not affect the color. Clean up as soon as possible after an accident to prevent staining. Work the disinfectant well into the fibers of the carpet, using a small brush if necessary, and leave it for a few minutes to take effect.
- In the case of solid matter, remove as much as possible with a pooper-scooper or similar tool, and then disinfect thoroughly.

WHAT IS THE BEST WAY TO CLEAN UP AFTER A PUPPY WHEN IT HAS AN ACCIDENT IN THE HOME?

- This should not be a problem provided your dog had been house-trained and used to living in domestic surroundings at an earlier stage in his life. The dog may urinate around the house if he is not neutered, but this is territorial marking rather than a lapse in house-training.
- If it persists, you will need to have him neutered. Some dogs that have been in kennels, or shut in for long periods, may be reluctant to go outdoors to relieve themselves, especially when the weather is bad, so be alert to this. Give your dog plenty of opportunity to go outside, particularly when you first bring him home.

MY NEW DOG WAS IN A RESCUE SHELTER FOR A MONTH BEFORE WE ACQUIRED HIM. WILL HE BE CLEAN IN THE HOME?

HOW CAN I MAKE SURE THAT MY PUPPY DOES NOT DEFECATE RANDOMLY AROUND THE BACKYARD?

- The simplest way is to obtain a spray from a pet supply store that will attract your dog to the desired location.
- Choose a part of the yard away from the house that can be hygienically cleaned without difficulty.
- A paved area is much easier to clean and disinfect than a lawn. Keep clear of where children may play, because of the slight risk that they could come into contact with roundworm eggs.

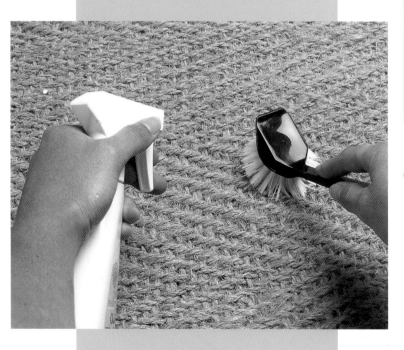

SHOULD I SCOLD THE PUPPY WHEN IT HAS AN ACCIDENT INDOORS?

● There is no point in scolding your puppy unless you catch it in the act. The pup will not understand what it has done wrong, and your scolding may confuse the training process. Rubbing the puppy's nose in the puddle is equally ineffective and is likely to upset your pet.

● A lapse of house-training could have happened because you were less alert to the puppy's needs than usual.

● Clean up well, and try to avoid a recurrence.

● If you need to go out and can't take your puppy with you, don't withhold drinking water in the hope that this will prevent your pup from urinating during your absence; such a practice could seriously affect the young puppy's kidneys.

● Instead, confine the pup to an area that is easy to clean, and protect the floor with a thick layer of newspaper on top of a plastic bag.

● Try not to leave your puppy for long periods, however, because it is likely to become distressed.

- This is likely, especially once a female dog is mature, because her urine is more acidic than that of a male dog. The risk is also higher during periods of dry weather, when there is no rain to dilute the urine.

- Train your dog to urinate either on bare ground or on a solid concrete surface, where the long-term effects of the urine will be less evident. If she persists in using the grass, water the contaminated area thoroughly to minimize the consequences.

IS IS TRUE THAT A BITCH'S URINE WILL KILL THE GRASS?

WHAT IS THE BEST WAY TO CLEAN UP AFTER OUR DOG WHILE WE ARE WALKING IN A PARK?

- It is a legal obligation for dog owners to clean up after their pets in many public places, and containers are usually provided for the waste.

- There are various tools that you can purchase to make this task easier. Long handles that save bending can be especially useful for older owners.

- Choose a tool that is convenient to carry and easy to disinfect after use. Take a supply of plastic bags to help you dispose of the mess.

- Cleaning up after a dog creates a pleasanter environment, but it does not guarantee the removal of every trace of the feces or eliminate the risk of roundworms in the area used.

- You may have to wait until your puppy is about 6 months old before it asks to go out. Prior to this, your house should remain clean, provided you give the pup the opportunity to go out regularly during the day.

- Your puppy will quickly develop the habit of relieving itself when you take it to the required spot.

- Excitement resulting from a game can cause your puppy to urinate inadvertently in the home, but under normal circumstances, it will not soil here once it is used to going outside. If an accident does occur indoors, clean up thoroughly (see page 64), so that the puppy is not attracted back to the same spot.

- In the backyard, of course, this attraction has an advantage, because the puppy will reinforce its scent with repeated visits.

AT WHAT AGE WILL MY PUPPY ASK TO GO OUTSIDE WHEN IT WANTS TO RELIEVE ITSELF?

basic training

Training your pup to respond to simple commands, and accustoming it to wearing a collar and leash.

- Basic training can begin along with house-training, almost as soon as you arrive home with your pet. Encourage the puppy to sit before you place its food in front of it.
- The pup will probably not respond at first, but will soon sit almost instinctively. Show the puppy what is required by applying gentle pressure over its hindquarters, placing your thumb and finger on each side of its hips.
- Sitting is a natural posture for a dog, so it will adopt this position readily. You can reinforce with praise, and in the beginning, treats.
- Your puppy must also learn its name, so always call and talk to it by name.
- Before long, the pup will respond instinctively to your call.

WHEN SHOULD I BEGIN TO TRAIN MY PUPPY?

WHAT COMMANDS MUST MY DOG LEARN?

- It is essential that your dog learn to sit and to stay. This is a step-by-step process. Once your dog has learned to sit (see above), you can begin teaching it to stay.
- A retractable leash is useful for this.
- Let the leash out and walk away from your pup, watching it all the time and giving the command "Stay!" At first the puppy will instinctively run after you, so you will need to stop, make the pup sit, and repeat the exercise.
- Be patient in the early stages, because your puppy's natural exuberance will urge it to follow you. Proper leash training is vital, so that your dog does not persist in pulling ahead, but walks just behind you.
- In the interests of safety, the dog must sit at the edge of the sidewalk with you, and not rush forward into the street. You must keep the dog on a short leash in this situation.

HOW LONG SHOULD TRAINING SESSIONS LAST?

● Puppies have a relatively short concentration span, so keep formal training sessions to about 10 minutes. Choose a spot where there will be no distractions.

● It is important to make the training sessions fun, and provide your puppy with plenty of encouragement, especially when it reacts as required.

● Try to show your puppy as much as possible what is needed. It is helpful to have another person with you at first. He or she can stay with the puppy to help it feel less isolated and encourage it to do what you ask.

● Do not scold or punish the puppy if it fails to respond as required, because this is likely to confuse it. Instead, repeat the session several times each day, if possible, for short periods, and you should soon find that your puppy, in its eagerness to please, will start to respond positively.

HOW OFTEN SHOULD TRAINING SESSIONS BE REPEATED?

● You can then lavish it with praise, and reward it. Don't rely too heavily on treats, however, or your puppy will seek these rather than carrying out your requests.

● The more time you devote to training your puppy, the greater the likelihood that it will make rapid progress. But don't neglect the basic lessons once they have been mastered.

● Incorporate them into more advanced training routines to help the young dog build on its existing knowledge of what is required. It is also a good idea to include other family members in the training process, so that as the puppy grows older, it will respond readily to their commands also.

● Opinion among professional dog trainers is divided on the use of choke collars. They can undoubtedly assist in cases where dogs persistently pull ahead, slouch behind, or otherwise refuse to walk properly on the leash. The collar tightens around the dog's neck, causing discomfort until the dog starts to walk again at your pace. There is a risk of injury, however, unless the collar is fitted correctly. You must first remove the dog's regular collar, and then loop the choke collar so that it will slacken when pressure is relaxed on the leash to which it is attached.

● An alternative to the choke collar is a device that fits first over the dog's nose, like a horse's noseband and then around its neck. This controls the dog's head movements.

SHOULD I USE A CHOKE COLLAR?

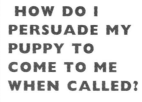

HOW DO I PERSUADE MY PUPPY TO COME TO ME WHEN CALLED?

● Provided you called your puppy by name from the beginning, it should instinctively respond when called during training routines in your home and yard.

● Greater difficulties may arise when the puppy is allowed off the leash, and there are interesting scents to distract it. Your calls may then be ignored, at least for a while.

● Be patient, and always reinforce the bond between you by making a fuss over your puppy when it returns to you after being called. This appeals to the dog's pack instincts, which encourage it to remain in contact with members of the family group.

● The collar should be fitted almost as soon as you acquire your puppy, partly because it carries an identification tag for use if the pup gets lost.

● You can connect a leash to the collar for brief training sessions from about the age of 10 weeks. The puppy is likely to resent having its freedom constrained in this way, and may pull badly at first.

● Choose a leash that feels comfortable in your hand, and is suitable for your dog; a large breed will need a stronger leash. Some leashes incorporate fluorescent material, which can be a valuable safety feature when you walk your dog at night on dark streets.

WHEN SHOULD MY PUPPY BEGIN TO WEAR A COLLAR AND LEASH?

out & about

Training your puppy at an early stage means it can be safely let off the leash.

AT WHAT STAGE SHOULD I LET MY PUPPY OFF THE LEASH WHEN WE ARE OUT FOR A WALK?

- This depends partly on the progress of your puppy's training, but generally by six months of age, the young dog should be able to run freely in safe locations away from traffic and farm animals.
- The risk is that once your dog realizes it can explore on its own, it may be reluctant to return to you—simply because its curiosity gets the better of it.
- Use an extendable leash as an interim measure to allow the puppy greater freedom. Then when it is finally let off the leash, your pup is less likely to run far.

HOW DO I ENCOURAGE MY PUPPY TO WALK IN A STRAIGHT LINE AND NOT PULL AHEAD?

- Use a wall or fence to help you in the early stages of training. Keep the puppy "sandwiched" between you and the barrier, so that it can't pull away from you at an angle. Try at all times to keep the puppy walking on your left side, just behind you.
- That is why the expression "Heel!" is used when a dog tries to pull ahead. Your pet will find it easier to respond in its home environment than out on the street, where it may lag behind—to sniff at a lamppost, for example.

WHY IS IT MORE DIFFICULT TO TRAIN SOME DOGS THAN OTHERS?

- Amenability to training depends upon the dog's breed and background.
- Sporting dogs, such as retrievers and spaniels, that are used to working one-on-one with people, are likely to be the most responsive to training.
- Problems most often arise with dogs that have a relatively independent lifestyle, such as Beagles and other pack hounds.
- Although affectionate and friendly by nature, these dogs will follow a scent with great determination and are not generally responsive under these circumstances.
- They tend to relate better to other dogs, however, because of their social natures.

IS IT HARDER TO TRAIN AN OLDER DOG THAN A PUPPY?

- Puppies are much better learners than older dogs, but it is possible, with patience, to teach an older individual successfully.
- It will be easier if the dog has previously experienced some proper training, which will give you a base to build on.
- Bear in mind that mature male dogs especially are likely to be more assertive, which can create problems. Female dogs and neutered dogs of both sexes are apt to respond more readily to training.
- A similar routine to that recommended for puppies should suffice when house-training or obedience training an older dog.

WHAT SHOULD I DO IF MY DOG RUNS AWAY?

- Always try to watch where your dog is, and call it back to you at frequent intervals, especially if it appears to be straying. If the dog suddenly bounds away, don't chase it.
- Your dog will see this as a game, and will probably continue running, and you will be unlikely to catch up with it. Instead, stand your ground, and call the dog back to you. It can be helpful to train your dog to respond to the sound of a high-pitched dog whistle.
- Although the whistle is inaudible to human ears, the sound carries a long distance and is detected by the dog's more sensitive hearing.
- If all else fails, head back to your car, where it is possible that you may find your dog waiting for you.

social training

Help your dog to become socially acceptable and master obedience skills.

HOW DO I STOP MY PUPPY FROM CHEWING MY HAND?

- A puppy instinctively uses its mouth to explore the texture of objects, including a person's hand. It is unlikely to bite, but in the excitement of a game, it may nip your skin with its sharp teeth. Don't allow your pup to play with your hand, because this behavior can become a habit, and the dog may bite harder as it grows older.
- If your puppy begins to grab your hand when you are playing together, stop and make a point of removing your hand and scolding the pup. It will then soon realize that it should not behave in this way.
- You can also provide the puppy with a chew toy instead.

HOW DO I PERSUADE THE PUPPY TO GIVE UP ITS TOY?

- You need to teach your puppy to drop the toy on command. This is an important lesson for the young dog to learn at an early stage to prevent it from becoming over-possessive and biting when you attempt to take an object away from it. Stop the game, place your left hand across your puppy's upper jaw, and pry down the lower jaw with your right hand (reverse your grip if you are left-handed), while giving the command "Drop!"
- The toy will fall out of the dog's mouth, and you can retrieve it. Before long, your puppy should drop its ball when commanded, allowing the game to continue. Some dogs, such as retrievers, instinctively behave in this manner, having been bred over many generations to retrieve game and drop it on command.

- Consistency from the outset is important. Don't allow your puppy to sit on the sofa, and then expect it not to climb on chairs when it is older.
- If the dog has not been allowed on the sofa, and has its own bed in the room, it should not jump up. Allow the dog into this room only when you are present, and it should not misbehave. If you find your dog on a sofa, tell it to get down then put it in another room.

HOW SHOULD I
TRAIN MY
DOG NOT TO
DAMAGE
FURNITURE
AND CHEW
ITEMS
AROUND THE
HOME?

- This kind of damage typically occurs when a puppy is teething, up to 6 months of age. Try to distract your dog's attention by providing a range of chews and other items that can be gnawed. Supervision is also important, since a bored dog is more likely to behave in this way than one that has company.
- If you must leave your dog alone, don't allow it to roam around the home, but confine it to an area where less damage is likely to occur. Bear in mind that dogs are not discriminatory. They may gnaw electric cords and run the risk of electrocution. If you find your puppy with a cord in its mouth, switch off the appliance before attempting to remove the cord, or you could both be electrocuted.
- Take care with appliances that are left permanently running, such as refrigerators or aquarium equipment. Check that the cords are out of your dog's reach.

WHY DO DOGS ATTACK FARM ANIMALS? HOW DO I TRAIN MY DOG SO THAT IT WILL NOT HARASS SHEEP?

● Dogs that run in packs often develop a pack mentality, an attitude that probably goes back to their wolf ancestors. However, these domestic dogs will chase sheep, cattle, or horses for sport, not because they are hungry.

● Some farm dogs that are raised around livestock will tour calving and lambing sheds to find afterbirths to eat, but these dogs won't chase stock.

● If you live or exercise your dog in a rural environment, be sure to keep it on leash when near livestock. If seen harassing a rancher's stock, your dog's life is at risk, and you are subject to strict laws that protect this stock.

● Up to the age of about 12 weeks, mixing with other dogs is inadvisable because of the risk of transmission of infection.

● Keeping a puppy in strict isolation with only human company on a long-term basis, however, is not a good idea.

● Allowing a young dog to socialize with others in public places should make it less nervous and better able to communicate effectively with other dogs. Dogs often meet up regularly when out for walks and may enjoy playing together.

IS IT A GOOD IDEA TO ALLOW MY PUPPY TO SOCIALIZE WITH OTHER DOGS?

- They can be very useful, especially if you have not owned a puppy before. The classes will give you the opportunity to discuss any individual training problems with an experienced trainer, and teach your pet how to interact with other dogs.
- This is an important skill, especially once the dog is let off the leash and likely to come into contact with other dogs out of their owners' reach.
- Ask for information about classes in your area from your veterinarian or a local dog club. Most are open to young dogs aged six months and up. You will probably need to sign up for a course well in advance, because the number of places is likely to be limited.
- Once your dog has mastered the basic skills, you may want to participate in a more advanced course, possibly leading to obedience competitions.

- Many dogs behave in this way. It is often a sign of excitement or attention-seeking, but it needs to be discouraged since the dog's claws could inflict a painful scratch, or snag clothing. As soon as it behaves in this way, take hold of your puppy's front legs close to the shoulder, and put them down gently onto the ground, giving the command "No!"
- Before long, your puppy should stop the behavior.
- Adopt the same procedure if the puppy tries to stand on your knees when you are sitting down, or attempts to stand up on a counter.

HOW SHOULD I STOP OUR GREAT DANE PUPPY FROM JUMPING UP ON PEOPLE?

- One of the joys of owning a dog is the bond that grows between you and your pet.
- Professional trainers can be helpful, especially if you have a difficult behavior problem with your dog, but routine training is best done by the people who will be involved in the dog's daily life. Persuading the dog to transfer its loyalties from its trainer to you could create additional difficulty.
- If you plan to show your dog competitively, however, you may want to employ a professional handler who is used to getting the best from a dog under these circumstances.

WOULD IT BE BETTER TO EMPLOY A PROFESSIONAL TRAINER?

The amount of exercise a dog needs is dictated partly by its origins; for example, hounds are naturally much more active than lap dogs. Dogs benefit most from regular exercise each day, rather than long periods on weekends. Try to stick to a routine while exercising your dog or it will become restless and constantly follow you around in anticipation of a walk.

5 Exercise

Young dogs, especially large breeds, need to be exercised cautiously, to prevent damage to their joints early in life. To protect them, they should never be allowed to run off the leash until they are fully trained. Extendable leashes that can be played out in suitable areas will give young dogs an opportunity to exercise even at a stage when they cannot be allowed to run by themselves.

first steps

Walking your dog and equipping it with a suitable leash or harness.

HOW MANY WALKS DO DOGS REQUIRE EACH DAY?

- Dogs should be walked at least once a day, unless they live in spacious surroundings, such as a farm, where they can obtain plenty of exercise for themselves.
- If you have time, you can take your puppy out two or three times during the day. This will add interest and enjoyment to the puppy's life and help to satisfy its curiosity about the world around it.
- Try to choose different routes to allow your puppy to learn more about its home environment.

HOW FAR SHOULD I WALK WITH MY PUPPY?

- Once your puppy has completed its vaccinations, you can begin taking it out for brief walks.
- Don't take the puppy on a long hike, which could result in damage to its developing joints, bones and muscles, especially in larger breeds.
- Relatively short but regular walks will maintain the puppy's fitness, and an extendable leash will allow it to explore safely.
- Don't allow your puppy or dog off the leash until it is properly trained and unlikely to run off alone.

● In terms of everyday living, a collar is fine for all dogs, but when the dog walks on a leash, the collar can create pressure on the vertebral column in its neck or on its trachea.

● The small breeds are better exercised using a harness, which places less stress on the neck area.

● Choose a harness of suitable size with adjustable straps; dogs appear to find leather straps most comfortable.

● If your dog is actively aggressive toward others, you must muzzle it, especially if it is to be allowed off the leash.

● Ex-racing Greyhounds should always be muzzled, because although they are not instinctively aggressive, they will chase much smaller dogs, and can harm them.

● Choose a muzzle that is easy to fit, and will remain secure.

MY DOG CAN BE AGGRESSIVE TOWARD OTHER DOGS. SHOULD I MUZZLE HIM? IF SO, WHAT IS THE BEST TYPE OF MUZZLE TO USE?

Metal muzzles may be more durable than plastic but are slightly heavier.

● It is important, however, to discover why your dog is acting aggressively; neutering can sometimes reduce such instincts, as can behavior modification by an expert trainer.

play safe

Ensuring your dog is safe when walking in the countryside or on a beach.

IS IT SAFE TO TAKE MY DOG FOR A WALK ON THE BEACH?

- Check first that dogs are not banned from the beach. This is most likely in popular locations, and bans are often seasonal.
- Your dog must not be allowed to run about and upset other visitors to the beach; keep it on its leash if you have any doubts about its behavior.
- Avoid areas where there may be tar that will contaminate your dog's coat.
- Don't allow your pet to run along a breakwater on its own, because a slip could prove fatal.
- If you plan to spend a day at the beach, be sure to take drinking water and a bowl for your dog.

ARE THERE ANY DANGERS TO WALKING IN THE COUNTRYSIDE?

● Avoid areas populated with livestock and wildlife that your dog might chase.
● When near these areas, keep your dog under strict leash control.
● Woodland can also be dangerous, partly because of the risk of snakes, but also because of the threat of Lyme disease, which is spread by ticks (see page 107) in many areas, especially where deer are prevalent.

ARE THERE ANY PRECAUTIONS THAT I SHOULD TAKE WHEN EXERCISING MY DOG DURING THE WINTER?

● If it is cold and wet, your dog may benefit from wearing a coat. This is especially important for Greyhounds and Whippets, which have thin coats and lack the body fat of other breeds.
● Choose a coat that is weather resistant and has a snug lining. Take your dog along to check the fit, or measure the dog in a straight line from the base of its tail to the neck. You may want to buy matching boots, or paw wax to help protect your dog's feet.
● It is important not to venture too far afield when the weather is bad, and a cellular phone can be useful for emergencies.
● If your dog runs across a frozen pond, don't be tempted to follow. A dog is much better able to survive in, and climb out of, freezing water than is a person.

IS IT REALLY DANGEROUS TO EXERCISE DOGS WHEN THE WEATHER IS HOT?

WHAT SHOULD I DO IF MY DOG DISAPPEARS?

- Dogs are usually as reluctant as people to rush around in the heat. They have greater difficulty than we do keeping cool, partly because of their thick coats, but also because they do not perspire as effectively as humans.
- Their sweat glands are confined to a small area between the toes, and their only other method of heat loss depends on the evaporation of fluid from their nasal cavities.
- The breeds at greatest risk from heat-stroke are those with greatly shortened noses, such as the Bulldog and Boxer. Be particularly careful when exercising them on hot days.

- Carry out a thorough search, retracing your steps as far as possible, and listen intently for sounds of your dog.
- If all else fails, report the loss of your dog to the local police. It is also helpful to inform animal welfare groups in your area.
- Notify local veterinarians, in case your dog is found injured and taken to one of them. An ID tag, tattoo, or microchip (see page 41) will assist its speedy return.
- If there is no news within a few days, consider contacting local newspapers or radio stations that may carry information about lost and found pets.

IS IT SAFE TO THROW STICKS FOR MY DOG TO CHASE?

● This cannot be recommended, because there is a slight but real risk that the stick could poke into the dog's eye, or splinter in its mouth.

● If you do throw a stick for your dog, you must choose a short, relatively fresh piece of wood, and throw it in such a way that it will fall to the ground before the dog is likely to reach it.

● It is safer to use a plastic flying disk that won't injure your dog.

● Toys intended for dogs to chase and return to you are an excellent way of exercising and training your pet. Teach the dog how to use the toy in your backyard first.

● Train your dog to drop the toy on command when it returns to you, and be sure to praise it.

● Be careful with toys that can be tugged. Pulling too hard could dislodge the teeth of a young puppy or an old dog.

● Don't allow your dog to become overexcited with tugging toys. It must be prepared to drop the toy when told.

IS IT A GOOD IDEA TO ENCOURAGE MY DOG TO CHASE AFTER TOYS?

extra exercise

Letting your dog run free, and swim as a form of exercise.

CAN I CHAIN MY DOG IN OUR LARGE BACKYARD TO GIVE IT MORE EXERCISE?

- This is feasible, but should not be done routinely. It is far better to fence the yard.
- Your dog will be vulnerable to the elements, and an event such as a sudden thunderstorm during your absence could cause it great distress.
- It is essential, in any case, to provide a dry kennel, where the dog can take shelter from heat and rain. A bowl of water within easy reach is also vital.
- Check that the tie stake is securely held in the ground, and does not work loose over time.
- Never leave a dog chained at the front of the house, where it could be teased by passersby.

ALTHOUGH MY DOG GOES OUT FOR REGULAR WALKS, SHOULD HE BE ALLOWED TO RUN FREE? THIS IS DIFFICULT BECAUSE WE LIVE IN A TOWN.

- Letting a dog off the leash allows it to be more active and gives it greater opportunity for exploration, but this is not essential as long as your dog receives enough exercise.
- You can judge this by noting if your dog settles down to sleep for a while after its walk, or it remains restless.
- An extendable leash (see page 70) is especially useful where safety considerations make it impossible for a dog to run on its own. As often as you can, take the dog somewhere it can walk freely, perhaps on the weekend.

- Dogs can swim, but they can't fight a strong current, so never allow your dog to enter the sea when it is rough, or to swim in areas where there is a strong undercurrent.
- Swimming is a good form of activity for dogs, and some breeds—notably those that retrieve game—are eager to enter the water.
- Avoid stagnant water, with its attendant smells, and beware of fast-flowing rivers and stretches of water from which your dog could not return easily to dry land. This applies particularly if your dog is a regular swimmer, because it is unlikely to recognize the danger before plunging in.

CAN MY DOG SWIM? IS THIS A GOOD FORM OF EXERCISE?

This is an aspect of dog care that needs to be considered when you are choosing a dog, because some dogs need considerably more grooming than others. It can increase the cost of keeping a dog if you have to use the services of a professional groomer to maintain your dog's coat in top condition.

6 Grooming

A wide range of grooming tools are available from pet stores and similar outlets. Regular grooming, especially during the two shedding periods each year, will help to keep the home cleaner because your dog will not be shedding its hair on the carpet and furnishings.

You will need nail clippers to keep your dog's nails neat and short to prevent injury from snagging and tearing nails on carpeting, fabrics, and objects outdoors.

When it comes to bathing your dog, there are many shampoos to choose from, some are medicated to protect against fleas and other external parasites. These will also remove your pet's natural odor, which can become quite strong in the home.

grooming routine

All you need to know about the grooming requirements for your dog.

HOW OFTEN IS IT NECESSARY TO GROOM OUR DOG?

- This depends on the age and breed of your dog, and to some extent on its lifestyle. Dogs that are often outdoors need much more grooming than those that stay mainly in the home. Longhaired dogs usually require daily grooming to prevent their coats from becoming matted, while shorthaired dogs can be combed and brushed once or twice a week to keep their hair in good condition.
- The dog's coat may also need to be trimmed occasionally. The inside of the spaniel's earflaps may harbor ear infections if not trimmed regularly.
- Breeds with thick coats, such as the Old English Sheepdog, may benefit from having their coats cut back in hot climates to help keep them cooler.

WHAT ARE THE BASIC TOOLS THAT I NEED FOR GROOMING MY DOG?

- A brush and comb are essential. A comb with revolving teeth is especially useful for a longhaired dog. It will not pull the hair like a conventional comb, and will tease out matted sections quite easily.
- Remove loose hairs with the comb or with a brush.
- A fine-toothed flea comb is likely to be useful. Cotton balls are helpful for wiping the area around the eyes and under the earflaps.
- Specialized tools can be added according to need. A hound glove, for example, fits over the hand and helps to give the dog's coat a good gloss as a final touch to grooming.

chamois sponge

soft brush

rubber brush

hound glove

wire comb

pastic comb

eye wipes and ear wipes

nail clippers

wire brush

toothbrush and paste

HOW MUCH DO
GROOMING
REQUIREMENTS
VARY
ACCORDING
TO INDIVIDUAL
BREEDS?

- They differ significantly, particularly in the case of show dogs, whose style of grooming may be an important part of the preparation for the ring. The dogs that are simplest to groom are those with short coats, including many hounds.
- Long-coated dogs need more grooming, and wire-haired breeds, such as the Airedale Terrier, may need their coats professionally stripped about every eight weeks to remove excess hair.

WHEN SHOULD I START TO GROOM MY DOG?

- You can begin grooming your puppy's coat soon after you acquire the dog. In the case of longhaired breeds, the coat will be far less profuse at this stage.
- Nevertheless, it helps to accustom the puppy to the sensation of being groomed, so that it will accept this attention later in life. Train your puppy to stand still for grooming, preferably with someone else to assist you.

DO SOME DOGS SHED LESS THAN OTHERS?

- Dogs with wire coats do not shed their hair, and excess hair must be stripped from their coats at least twice a year.
- Breeds that do not shed, such as Poodles, need to be clipped every six to eight weeks, which adds to the cost of keeping such breeds.
- Other dogs normally shed much of their longer, denser winter coat in the spring and early summer, and require more grooming at that time of year.
- The fur then regrows to its full length in the fall.
- After neutering, however, dogs may sometimes shed their hair more heavily outside these seasons. This is thought to be because of hormonal changes.

WHAT SHOULD I DO IF MY DOG'S COAT BECOMES BADLY MATTED?

- The matted areas must be removed in case they become soiled, when they could easily harbor infection.
- Combing out the mats, even if possible, would be exceedingly painful, however, and your dog might subsequently refuse to be groomed again.
- The best approach is to cut the mats out carefully with a pair of blunt-ended scissors.
- Although this may disturb the smoothness of your dog's coat, the hair will soon regrow.

WHERE SHOULD I GROOM MY DOG?

- Groom your dog on a raised surface, so that you can reach it without bending and have easy access to the underside of its body.
- The best location is likely to be outside, on a table of convenient height.
- If outdoor grooming is not possible, select an area of your home which is easy to clean and where the lighting is good.

1 On the stomach, use a brush and work upward from the roots with firm, short strokes. Loosen any tangled or dead hair.

2 Start on the dog's back and work from the tail end, toward the head.

3 Hold the tail to one side, and gently but firmly brush the fore- and hindlimbs. Brush the tail thoroughly, working from the root to the tip.

4 Keeping the brush away from the dog's face, brush the neck and ears. Hold each ear, and groom beneath, teasing out any tangles with your fingers, then groom under the chin.

5 Using a comb rather than a brush, repeat the procedure to remove any remaining tangles.

6 When the grooming is complete, the dog should have a soft bushy undercoat, and a long straight topcoat.

● The first clip is usually given at around the age of three months. The puppy may be nervous about the procedure, and especially worries at the sound of the clippers, but this should soon pass when the dog realizes that it will not be hurt.

● If you have a pair of electric clippers at home, you can help the puppy become familiar with the noise, by running them just above its coat.

● Up to about 9 months of age, poodles are traditionally styled in a puppy clip: an even, allover trim that resembles the coat of a lamb.

● Many owners continue with this lamb clip, especially for white or black poodles.

● An alternative is the Dutch clip, where the hair on the legs is left longer than that of the body. The best-known style for Poodles is the lion clip, which was reportedly developed by the French queen Marie Antoinette, and is universally used for show purposes.

● The coat is left long from the head to the end of the rib cage, and the rest of the body is closely shaved, apart from the decorative pompoms present on the legs and the tail.

SHOULD I HAVE OUR DOG GROOMED PROFESSIONALLY?

● It can be a good idea to have your dog groomed and bathed professionally two or three times a year to keep it in prime condition.

● A professional groomer can assist with routine grooming or prepare dogs for the show ring, but standards can vary and the best way to find a good dog groomer is by recommendation.

● For everyday purposes, however, you should be able to groom your own dog without difficulty, and this can be a source of great satisfaction.

● This is certainly possible, as evidenced by the many grooming businesses in existence. The variety of styles required for different breeds means that there is much to learn, particularly if you want to show your dog.

● In the United States and most other countries, training courses are organized through a national grooming association. Contact the AKC for information, or ask a salon in your area if they would be willing to take you on and provide training.

● It is not just a matter of washing the dog and grooming it; you will need to be able to handle dogs—and their owners—in what can sometimes be fairly stressful situations.

● Nevertheless, this can be an absorbing career that gives you the opportunity to work with animals and possibly run your own business eventually.

CAN I MAKE A CAREER OUT OF DOG GROOMING?

bathing & drying

Whether or not to wash or bathe your dog, and drying its fur afterward.

AT WHAT AGE SHOULD MY DOG FIRST BE BATHED?

- Most dogs will not require a bath until they are about 6 months old.
- You may need to clean areas of the puppy's fur before this time, especially around the mouth, where food can mat the fur. This is particularly likely in the case of longhaired dogs and those fed on moist food.
- Avoid bathing the dog in cold or wet weather.

HOW OFTEN SHOULD I BATHE MY DOG?

- Dogs should be bathed only when necessary. If the dog is groomed frequently, bathing may be needed only a few times a year.
- Dogs that require bathing before dog shows are an exception. Wash the dog's bedding at the same time.
- Your dog may not appreciate your attentions, however, and you may need to prevent it from rolling in the dirt to alter its scent. If it gets dirty, wash it again without delay. This will not be harmful, although excessive bathing will strip the natural oil from the coat, and make it less water-resistant.
- A number of breeds, such as Labrador Retrievers, can simply shake their coats dry after venturing into water, partly because of this oily protection.

HOW SHOULD I BATHE THE DOG?

- It helps if you can bathe your dog outside. Use a plastic tub of suitable size. It is preferable not to utilize your own bathtub for hygienic reasons.
- If this is unavoidable, place a rubber mat in the tub to keep your dog from slipping and from scratching the tub with its claws.
- Half-fill the tub with tepid water, and prepare all the equipment you need: a container for pouring water over your dog, a plastic apron to protect yourself, and some dog shampoo.

- Lift your dog into the tub and pour water over it, starting toward the rear. You may need someone to help you hold the dog at first, in case it becomes upset.
- Thoroughly soak the coat with water.
- Work the shampoo into the coat according to the label recommendations.
- Wash the head last, and take care that the shampoo does not get into the dog's eyes.
- Lift the dog out of the tub for a few moments while you drain away the dirty water.
- Half-fill the tub with clean water, and rinse the shampoo out of the dog's coat.
- If there is a convenient faucet, a hand nozzle can be useful for this.

WHAT ABOUT ACTUALLY WASHING MY DOG?

WHAT ABOUT DRYING MY DOG AFTERWARD— CAN I USE A HAIR DRYER?

- After you lift your dog out of its bath, stand back, because the dog will probably shake itself. This is especially likely in breeds that enter water readily and whose coats are water-repellent.
- It is an efficient way for a dog to dry off, and if the weather is warm, this natural air-drying is all that is needed.
- In colder conditions, you can rub your dog down with an old towel to prevent it from getting chilled.
- A hair dryer can be used, but only on a cool setting and provided the noise does not disturb your pet.

HOW DO I REMOVE MUD FROM MY DOG'S COAT AND SHOULD I WASH ITS FEET AFTER A WALK?

- Everyday washing is not recommended, because it will ultimately strip the oil from the dog's coat.
- Dry your dog's feet as much as possible, using an old towel, and wipe off any loose mud from the legs at the same time.
- Then wait until the mud dries on the hair, and comb or brush it out.

finishing touches

The best way to care for your dog's ears, eyes, nails, dewclaws, and teeth.

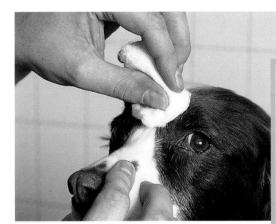

SHOULD I CLEAN MY DOG'S EARS REGULARLY?

- This is not essential unless your dog has heavy, pendulous ears. In these dogs, the entrance to the ear canal is more likely to become blocked, making it easier for fungi and bacteria to multiply and cause infection.
- Clean beneath the earflaps with cotton balls, and trim back excess hair regularly. Never probe the ear canal with a cotton swab, which could cause pain and injury to your pet.

- Breeds with compact faces, such as the Pug, are especially prone to this problem.
- It occurs when the compression of the face causes a blockage of the naso-lacrimal, or tear duct, with the result that instead of draining properly, tear fluid overflows from the eye and runs down the face.
- Bathe the affected areas with damp cotton balls, and consult with your veterinarian to see if the drainage can be improved.
- Surgery may be needed in severe cases.

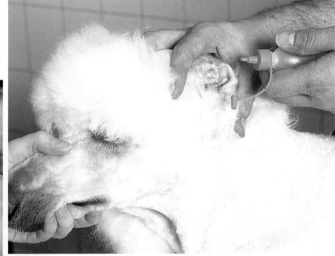

- You can purchase nail clippers from a pet store or pet supply catalog. Scissors may not be strong enough and could cause the nail to splinter, especially in larger breeds.
- Guillotine-style clippers are the best choice if you are unused to cutting a dog's claws, because they enable you to position the blade very accurately on the nail.
- First examine the dog's claws, and locate the pinkish area that extends a short distance down the claw.
- This reveals the path of the blood supply. It is vital to clip some distance beyond this area, where the tissue is dead, to guarantee that the procedure is painless. If by accident bleeding occurs, gentle pressure on the cut end should stem it rapidly.

WHAT TOOL IS BEST TO CUT MY DOG'S NAILS AND HOW SHOULD I CARRY OUT THIS TASK?

- Dogs that are reasonably active may not need their claws cut regularly, since these will wear down naturally through contact with hard surfaces, such as pavements.
- The dewclaws, however, need to be cut back every six to eight weeks.
- If left untrimmed, they can curl around, get caught and break, or penetrate the pad behind.
- Cut the dewclaw in exactly the same way as the other claws This is often an easier task, since the dewclaw is generally more accessible.
- If your dog has dark claws, which make it harder to detect the blood supply, be extra cautious to minimize the risk of bleeding.

MY DOG STILL HAS ITS DEWCLAWS. PLEASE ADVISE ON CLIPPING THESE BACK.

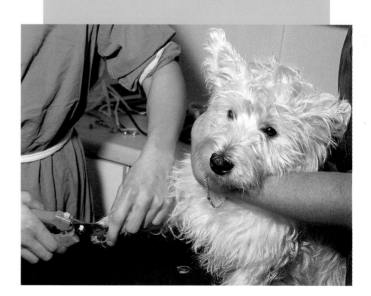

- Regular toothbrushing should begin when your dog is a puppy, although you are likely to need some assistance at first.
- Hold your dog, and open its mouth only as much as necessary. You can clean the teeth from the side, which is where tartar is most likely to accumulate.

WHAT IS THE BEST WAY TO CLEAN THE DOG'S TEETH?

- Use a toothbrush at first, to avoid being bitten, but later you may prefer a finger brush, which you can rub directly over your dog's teeth. Brush carefully to avoid causing your dog any discomfort.
- There is no need to rinse your dog's mouth afterward.
- Chews can be useful to help prevent the buildup of plaque.
- If your dog is already suffering from dental disease, however, or refuses to allow you to clean its teeth, your veterinarian may need to sedate it for this purpose.

SHOULD I BRUSH MY DOG'S TEETH REGULARLY? IF SO, WHAT SHOULD I USE?

- Dental care is important to prevent your dog from losing its teeth unnecessarily later in life. Dogs suffer far fewer dental cavities than humans do, but they are much more vulnerable to gum disease (gingivitis).
- This causes reddening of the gum, and is likely to lead to gum erosion and weakening of the teeth. Some breeds, such as Poodles, and Toy breeds, appear to be more prone to dental problems than others.
- Dogs that eat canned food are considered to be more vulnerable than those fed on a dry diet, because their teeth accumulate more tartar.
- Toothbrush kits for dogs are available from veterinary offices and pet stores. Don't use regular toothpaste, because dogs dislike it and will resist it.

Advances in veterinary care have helped to ensure that dogs are now living longer than ever before. The killer diseases of the past have been supplanted by vaccination programs, but it is vital to maintain your dog's protection through regular boosters. Illnesses of old age, such as chronic renal failure are now more commonly seen in

7 Health & disease

dogs attending veterinary clinics. Although it is impossible to reverse these illnesses of old age, careful dietary management, together with regular veterinary checks, will ensure that a dog has a good quality of life for as long as possible.

Because of advances in surgical and medical techniques, even disease such as cancer may be treated successfully. The chances of recovery are greatly increased by early diagnosis, while canine health insurance can deal with unexpected and costly veterinary expenses.

veterinarians

*Choosing a suitable veterinarian to look after your dog,
and deciding on home visits or the veterinarian's office.*

DOES IT MATTER IF I DON'T SEE THE SAME VETERINARIAN EVERY TIME?

- For most of your dog's life, you may visit the practice only for an annual checkup and vaccinations, and it is not likely to matter that you see a different veterinarian each time.
- If your dog is undergoing a complex course of treatment, however—following surgery, for example—most practices should provide continuity of treatment from the same veterinarian.
- If this is not possible, computerized and other precise records should guarantee that a doctor seeing your dog for the first time during its treatment is fully apprised of its condition.

HOW DO I CHOOSE A VETERINARIAN?

- Although most veterinary colleges have similar curriculums, there may be practices and individuals who have special interests, talents, and abilities. Ask your pet-owning friends for recommendations.
- Don't overlook a nearby practice in favor of a fancy animal hospital across town.
- To choose a veterinarian, call for an appointment to visit him or her in person. Take notes as you ask questions about your dog's care, emergency capabilities, and special knowledge that he or she might have. Tour the hospital and note the equipment being used.
- Discuss fees for procedures you are contemplating, such as spaying or neutering your dog.

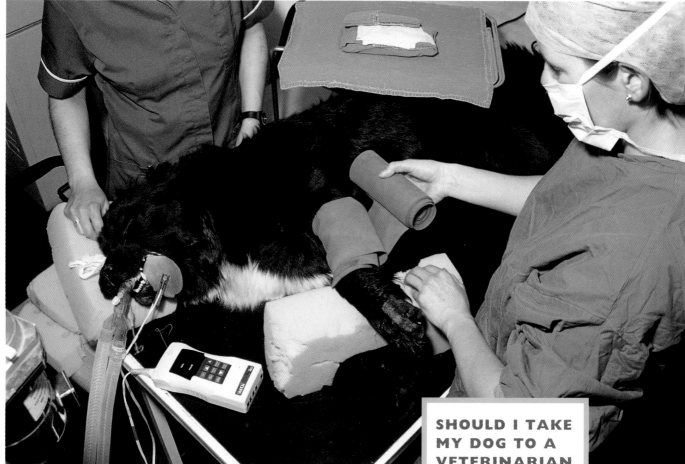

MY DOG IS SUFFERING FROM DIARRHEA, BUT APPEARS LIVELY. HOW LONG SHOULD I WAIT BEFORE CONTACTING THE VETERINARIAN?

- Because of their scavenging habits, dogs will occasionally eat food that causes minor digestive upsets. Provided your pet remains alert, avoid feeding it for 24 hours.
- Follow this with a bland diet of chicken and rice, complete with a probiotic (see page 60) to calm the gut and restore its bacterial balance.
- Give your dog free access to drinking water throughout, because it is likely to be dehydrated. If there is no improvement after this treatment, or your dog's condition deteriorates, seek veterinary advice without delay.
- Consult your veterinarian immediately in the case of a young puppy with diarrhea, because pups can dehydrate very rapidly, and fluid therapy may be needed.

SHOULD I TAKE MY DOG TO A VETERINARIAN OR ASK FOR A HOME VISIT IF SHE IS ILL?

- In almost all cases, unless advised by your veterinarian to the contrary, it will be better to take your dog to the veterinarian's office, where it can be thoroughly examined with all the necessary equipment.
- All veterinarians will see an emergency case in the office at short notice, whereas it can be difficult for a doctor to leave the office quickly for a house call. Some veterinarians provide a round-the-clock service, but even so, it will be less costly and better for your dog to be examined at the office.
- The only exception may be the case of a very sick elderly dog.

vaccinations

Outlines which vaccinations your puppy needs, and the best time to administer them.

- Vaccinations should be administered to most puppies by or shortly after six weeks of age. A booster is then given two to four weeks later. Your puppy's vaccinations depend on its age, health, the area in which you live, and endemic diseases that are prevalent in that region.
- There is no formula that fits every dog. Take the vaccination certificate that you received with the puppy to your veterinarian on your first visit. Annual boosters are generally required throughout the dog's life to maintain the necessary level of protection.

AT WHAT STAGE SHOULD MY PUPPY RECEIVE ITS VACCINATIONS?

WHAT DISEASES DO THE VACCINES USUALLY COVER?

- The initial vaccines protect your dog from distemper, hepatitis, leptospirosis, parvovirus, and in some cases, coronavirus and kennel cough.
- Lyme disease also has a vaccine. These vaccines rarely cause dangerous reactions and they will protect your dog from potentially fatal diseases.
- Dogs living in high densities in cities are especially susceptible to these diseases. When booster vaccinations are scheduled, be sure to advise your veterinarian of any illness or stress that your pet is under, such as pregnancy or heavy training.

ARE ANY SPECIAL VACCINATIONS LIKELY TO BE NEEDED?

- Rabies is a fatal disease that can affect all warm-blooded animals, including humans.
- Because of the public health significance of this disease, vaccination is required in the United States and some foreign countries.
- It is usually not required until the dog is four to six months of age, and is repeated annually, every two years, or every three years, depending on the vaccine used.

A veterinarian gives a 12-week-old Labrador puppy a vaccination.

general health

How to check for signs that your dog may be ill.

- A sick dog will lose its enthusiasm for life and often its appetite. It may drink more than usual and sleep for longer periods.
- Make a list of all the symptoms before consulting with your veterinarian.
- Try to be as precise as possible.
- Note the actual amount your dog is drinking by using a measuring cup to fill its bowl.
- Don't hesitate to seek help if you suspect that your dog is ill, because its condition could worsen rapidly.

MUST MY DOG'S NOSE BE WET FOR IT TO BE HEALTHY?

- Fluid from the lateral glands in a dog's nose lubricates the external part of the nostrils and makes them shiny. As a result, a moist nose is generally believed to be a sign of a healthy dog, but this is not invariably true.
- A dog that has slept in a hot place may have a dry nose on waking, because of slight dehydration. Once the dog cools down and has a drink, the nose will soon look moist again.
- Dogs that have suffered from distemper early in life, however, may have permanently dry noses because of the infection's long-term effect on the nasal glands.

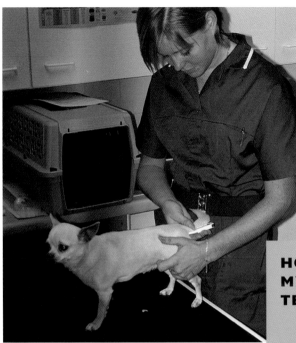

HOW DO I TAKE MY DOG'S TEMPERATURE?

- Have someone hold the dog still. Lubricate the bulb of the thermometer carefully with petroleum jelly and slide it a short way into the dog's rectum.
- Keep it in place for about two minutes. Withdraw the thermometer and read the figure.
- Clean it and shake it down as necessary for future use.

HOW CAN I FIND THE DOG'S PULSE?

- A pulse can be detected at various points on the dog's body, but the femoral artery, located on the inside of either hind leg, is usually preferred.
- You may need practice to locate it easily.
- Place your fingertips gently over the spot to detect the beat.

specific ailments

Discusses health problems that occur commonly in dogs.

HOW DO DOGS PICK UP GRASS SEEDS?

- Green grass seeds present no danger but once they ripen, they can resemble sharp splinters. Dogs can pick up the seedheads from relatively long grass that was not cut while it was flowering.
- The seed is most likely to penetrate between the pads as the dog walks and is forced through the skin. It then becomes very painful, and it may be too late for the dog to be able to pull it out with its teeth.
- Always suspect a grass seed if your dog develops sudden signs of lameness during or after a walk, and starts to chew ferociously at one of its feet. Don't look for the seed yourself, because the pain is likely to cause even the calmest dog to bite.
- Seek veterinary help to remove the seed before it travels more deeply into the body.

Ripe green grass seeds can present a problem for your dog.

IS THERE ANY OTHER REASON THAT MAY CAUSE MY DOG TO CHEW AT ITS PAW?

- Parasites known as chiggers or harvest mites could be to blame. They are the larval form of minute red spiders.
- The tiny larvae lodge between the dog's toes, although not all the paws may be affected. Treatment is simple, but chiggers (Trombicula autumnalis) are most active just when grass seeds are drying, so careful examination by your veterinarian may be needed to determine the cause of the dog's irritation.

Checking a dog's paw for chiggers.

IS THERE SOMETHING WRONG WITH MY DOG'S DIET? IT SEEMS TO SUFFER REGULARLY FROM EPISODES OF DIARRHEA.

- Sudden changes in diet can have this effect, especially in small dogs. Alterations in routine may also be implicated.
- Your dog's diet may be too rich, in which case a gradual switch to canned food with a higher cereal than meat content could be advantageous.
- Provide the dog with a bland chicken and rice diet during its recovery from an episode of diarrhea.
- If the problem persists, and especially if there is any sign of blood associated with the diarrhea, contact your veterinarian.

ARE SOME BREEDS MORE PRONE TO TUMORS THAN OTHERS?

- Among purebred dogs, Boxers (below) are one of the breeds susceptible to tumors of all types.
- Other breeds that appear to have a relatively high incidence of tumors include Boston Terriers and Cocker Spaniels.

WHY ARE FEMALE DOGS MORE PRONE TO URINARY INFECTIONS THAN MALES?

- This is essentially because the urethra—the canal that carries urine from the bladder to the outside—is shorter in female than in male dogs. As a result, bacteria can reach the female's bladder more easily.
- The greater acidity of the bitch's urine may also be more apt to trigger a urinary tract infection.

● Pancreatic insufficiency is a malfunction of the pancreas, a gland that is located close to the small intestine. It produces various hormones, which act as chemical messengers in the body, and enzymes that are directly responsible for the breakdown of foodstuffs in this part of the intestinal tract. In cases of pancreatic insufficiency, the enzymatic output is low, so that the food is not broken down properly and the dog produces pale-colored feces.

● Since the dog can't absorb its food adequately, weight loss is inevitable.

● The condition can be stabilized by the addition of enzymes in powdered or capsule form to the dog's food. An affected dog will frequently remain thin, although otherwise healthy.

● Pancreatic insufficiency is often associated with German Shepherd Dogs.

MY DOG IS VERY THIN AND MY VETERINARIAN SAYS THAT IT COULD BE SUFFERING FROM PANCREATIC INSUFFICIENCY —WHAT IS THIS?

● Studies suggest that four dogs in every thousand are likely to suffer from tumors each year, and older dogs between 7 and 10 years of age are most vulnerable to malignant (cancerous) tumors.

● The skin is the most common site of tumors, and if you detect any unexplained lumps on your dog's body, you should seek veterinary advice.

● Mammary tumors are also common, as are bone tumors in the large breeds. Treatment has advanced considerably over recent years, although early diagnosis is a key factor in determining the likelihood of a successful outcome.

● Surgery can be useful to excise mammary tumors. In other parts of the body, cryosurgery may be preferable. This entails freezing the diseased tissue and allowing it to slough off in due course.

● Chemotherapy and radiotherapy may also be used in certain cases.

HOW COMMON ARE TUMORS IN DOGS, AND WHAT TREATMENTS ARE AVAILABLE?

MY DOG MAY NEED TO HAVE ONE OF ITS LEGS AMPUTATED. WILL IT BE ABLE TO MANAGE ON THE OTHER THREE?

● It is surprising how well a dog can recover from the loss of a leg, and how little this affects its agility and quality of life, particularly once the muscles around the missing limb strengthen.

● It is especially important to make sure that your dog does not become overweight, because of its reduced support.

parasites

How to spot indicators that your dog is affected by parasites, and how to treat these conditions.

- A dog that is afflicted by fleas will bite repeatedly at its skin, particularly around the base of the tail where fleas often congregate.
- Red patches on the skin, where the dog has scratched, and tiny dark specks in the hair are additional indicators. Lice cause relatively few problems, but they can be present in puppies.
  - Look for the eggs, known as nits, attached to individual hairs.
  - Areas of hair loss may indicate the presence of mites on the dog's body.

HOW CAN I DETECT SIGNS OF FLEAS OR OTHER SKIN PARASITES?

- Use a flea comb when grooming your dog, because these parasites are too small to be captured by an ordinary comb.
- Pour some water into a disposable container, such as a yogurt container, and tip any fleas that you catch into the water, so that they cannot escape.
- A high-tech alternative is a stun comb that knocks the flea out and pauses to allow you to remove the flea from the dog's coat.
- External flea traps don't control fleas on your dog, but are intended to catch any of the parasites that have hatched around the home and are seeking a host.

WHAT IS THE BEST WAY TO CAPTURE AND REMOVE FLEAS?

WHAT IS THE BEST WAY OF TREATING FLEAS?

- Sprays, powders, and products that inhibit flea growth can be used. Powders are quick-acting and valuable for treating large numbers of fleas.
- Insect growth regulators block a critical part of the flea's development and are useful in the longer-term prevention of an infestation.
- All treatments must be applied not only to the dog but also to its environment to avoid reinfestation.
- Vacuum the floor close to the baseboard every day and wash the dog's bedding as an additional precaution.

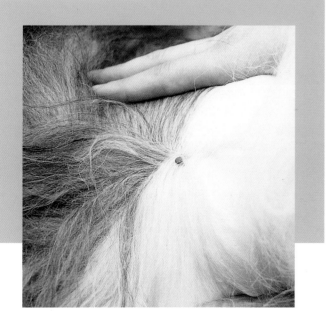

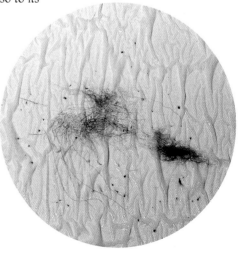

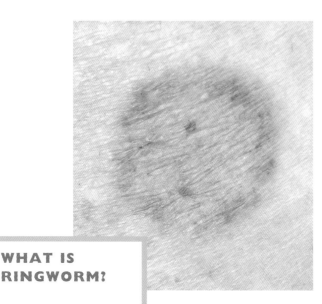

Ringworm lesion on human skin (left) closely resembles that found on dogs.

WHAT IS RINGWORM?

- Ringworm is caused by a parasitic fungus that infects the skin of dogs and results in circular patches of hair loss.
- The outer part of the circle is the most infectious. Ringworm is a zoonotic disease, meaning that it can spread to people, so affected dogs must be treated carefully. Ringworm in humans is typically revealed by circular red patches on the forearms, where the person has lifted an infected pet.
- If you suspect that your dog has ringworm, wash your hands thoroughly after handling it, using cold water, which will tend to close the skin pores and make it harder for the fungus to establish itself.

HOW IS HEARTWORM SPREAD?

- Heartworm infections have been found over the United States, including Alaska.
- The immature heartworms, known as microfilariae, are transmitted by biting insects, notably mosquitoes, which suck up these parasites with blood as they feed, and inject them into their next victim.
- The adult heartworms lodge in the heart and are difficult to treat, so dogs at risk of acquiring this infection are usually given prophylactic medication on a regular basis.

ARE THERE OTHER PARASITIC WORMS THAT CAN BE SPREAD TO DOGS THROUGH THEIR FOOD?

- There are a number of such parasites, but their distribution can be localized and their spread more easily controlled.
- The Echinococcus tapeworm, which begins its development in herbivores such as sheep, can infect dogs that eat the animals' raw meat. In New Zealand, where this infection is prevalent, deworming of dogs is compulsory.
- The giant kidney worm (Dioctophyma renale) is usually spread to dogs through raw fish. It is found, though rarely, in parts of the United States and mainland Europe, and not in Britain or Australia.

SHOULD I DEWORM MY DOG IF IT HAS FLEAS?

- If your dog has tapeworms and fleas simultaneously, the flea is probably the secondary host for the tapeworm.
- The tiny eggs of the tapeworm emerge from the anus in segments and stick to the hair.
- A feeding flea may then ingest one of these eggs, which starts to develop in its body. The irritated dog nibbles at its fur and can inadvertently swallow the flea, enabling the tapeworm to complete its development in the dog's intestinal tract.
- In this case, treating for tapeworms as well as for fleas is indicated.

Magnified picture of a tick with its head buried in a dog's skin.

ARE TICK-BORNE DISEASES A THREAT TO BOTH DOGS AND HUMANS?

- Lyme disease, the most common tick-carried disease in the United States, is caused by the spirochete *Borrelia burgdorferi*.
- Symptoms in dogs and humans include crippling arthritis, as well as neurological complications.
- Ask your veterinarian about Lyme disease vaccine. If you are in an area where the disease has been reported, your veterinarian will probably recommend that your dog be inoculated.

HOW CAN RINGWORM BE TREATED?

- Specific long-term antifungal therapy is required. The spores represent a continuing environmental hazard, and ongoing precautionary measures are needed to lessen the risk of other members of the household becoming infected.
- Disinfect grooming tools and bedding with an alcohol- or iodophor-based disinfectant.

HOW ABOUT OTHER PARASITES THAT MAY BE ENCOUNTERED?

- Dogs that are kept together in a kennel can be particularly vulnerable to parasites.
- Lungworms (*Filaroides osleri*) are commonly encountered in racing greyhounds. They lodge at the point where the trachea divides to enter the lungs and cause coughing after exercise.
- Whipworms, which are found in the cecum (a tiny pouch in the large intestine), can cause intermittent diarrhea.
- Hookworms can penetrate the underside of the dog's feet. They then migrate to the intestines, where they give rise to anemia. They are most frequently found in warmer parts of the United States and Europe.

Dogs kept together in a kennel can be particularly vulnerable to parasites.

infections & diseases

Useful information about symptoms, and treatment for common diseases in dogs.

WHAT IS THE DIFFERENCE BETWEEN THE TWO TYPES OF CANINE ADENOVIRUS?

COULD YOU GIVE ME SOME INFORMATION ABOUT DISTEMPER?

● Distemper is an acute and often fatal viral disease. Dogs that survive the initial infection often suffer permanent complications. Distemper is sometimes known as hardpad, because the virus can attack the skin of the pad, causing it to thicken. This effect also occurs on the exposed part of the nostrils. Distemper can also damage the enamel of the teeth, causing them to become rough and brownish. Fever, coughing, vomiting, and diarrhea are typical early symptoms. The virus localizes in the nervous system and may cause involuntary twitching of the facial muscles, and even convulsions. There is no treatment for this illness, although it may be possible to counter some of the effects on the nervous system.

● CAV-1 is the more serious form. It gives rise to the illness sometimes known as Rubarth's disease or infectious canine hepatitis (ICH). When ingested, the virus causes severe hepatitis. The liver becomes greatly enlarged and the symptoms of jaundice are evident, especially inside the mouth. The virus interferes with blood clotting and hemorrhages are likely. ICH is often fatal, and in dogs that recover, there may be permanent kidney damage. A transient bluish opacity that is apparent over the surface of the eyes during the recovery period gives the infection its other name of "blue eye."

The effects of CAV-2 are milder. This virus localizes in the respiratory tract and is a recognized cause of kennel cough (see page 42). CAV-1 may sometimes also attack the respiratory tract if it is inhaled, and in this case the resulting illness is apt to be less serious.

IS PARVOVIRUS STILL A THREAT?

● Parvovirus can still prove deadly, as it has since its sudden appearance in the 1970s. The effects of the virus differ according to the dog's age. Puppies that are under 5 weeks old when they are infected are likely to develop inflammation of the heart muscle, which can result in sudden death from cardiac failure. Pups that recover have permanently damaged hearts and are likely to die prematurely. In older dogs the virus attacks the lining of the intestinal tract, causing bloodstained diarrhea. Dehydration then becomes a serious threat to the dog's health, necessitating intensive fluid therapy. If the dog survives, the lining of its gut is usually permanently damaged, and loss of condition results from its inability to absorb nutrients efficiently. The dog may suffer repeated episodes of diarrhea as a result. Bleach (sodium hypochlorite) is a disinfectant recommended to destroy the parvovirus in your home. It is resistant to disinfectants and may survive in the environment for at least a year.

Leptospirosis is a urinary disease of many species of animals and is caused by a spirochete (a spiral-shaped bacterium). It is prevalent in areas inhabited by rodents, which act as reservoirs for the disease. It is spread by urinary contamination of water, which means that swimming dogs are more at risk than others. Jaundice is usually seen in affected dogs, together with fever, vomiting, and diarrhea. Treatment is usually successful, but often there is some permanent damage to the kidneys, and antibiotic therapy must be prolonged. Vaccines are available and of great value in prevention.

ARE SOME DOGS AT GREATER RISK FROM LEPTOSPIROSIS THAN OTHERS?

Rabies is usually spread by bites. The virus travels by way of the nerves, and dynamic signs do not appear until it reaches the brain. It may take weeks or months for outward signs to be seen. There are two types of rabies, dumb or paralytic, and furious. The first is less important, since an infected dog usually is not a threat to humans. In furious rabies, the dog displays aggressiveness, and may bite everything in its path. It can't swallow due to paralysis of its throat, and stringy, mucoid saliva drips from its mouth.

HOW WOULD I KNOW IF MY DOG HAD RABIES?

PLEASE GIVE ME SOME INFORMATION ON TOXOCARIASIS. WHAT ARE THE RISKS AND HOW CAN I PROTECT THE FAMILY?

It is possible to be infected by the rabies virus without being bitten. Close contact with an infected animal can cause cuts on your skin to become contaminated through its saliva. Wash the affected area thoroughly, using alcohol if possible, and apply iodine. Seek immediate medical aid—once clinical signs appear, recovery could be impossible. Rabies is endemic in every inhabited continent, apart from Australia, so don't pet stray dogs. A dog with rabies may appear friendly in the early stages of the infection and then bite unexpectedly.

WHAT SHOULD I DO IF I SUSPECT THAT I HAVE BEEN IN CONTACT WITH A RABID DOG?

The Toxocara eggs are voided from the dog's body in its feces but are not immediately infectious; they only become so after several days in the environment. Children who play in areas where dogs have soiled are at risk of contracting the infection by inadvertently transmitting the eggs to their mouths. Cases of this infection in humans are, however, rare. Preventive measures by dog owners and parents are essential, but it is almost impossible to eliminate Toxocara eggs from the environment, because they can survive for years, and wild animals, such as foxes, can also be a source of infection.

WHAT IS THE DANGER OF CHILDREN ACQUIRING TOXOCARIASIS IN PUBLIC PLACES?

This infection, caused by the roundworm Toxocara canis, is common in young puppies, which are often infected before birth by their mother and sometimes by their mother's milk. That is why it is so important to check females and possibly deworm prior to mating. The risk to young children stems from the Toxocara eggs, which they may ingest after playing with the puppy, by putting their fingers in their mouths or touching food without washing their hands. The eggs develop in the gut and cross into the bloodstream. The larvae may then spread to the eye and cause blindness. Regular deworming of your dog from an early age, together with teaching your children to wash their hands after touching their pet as well as before eating, should eliminate the risk.

how to treat

Administering treatments to your dog at home, and alternative medicine.

HOW DO I GIVE A PILL TO A DOG?

- Although there are pill guns for this purpose, it is not usually difficult to give a pill directly to a dog, provided it is used to having its mouth opened.
- Hold the dog's head up, placing your left hand across the muzzle, and pry down the lower jaw, keeping the head as vertical as possible.
- Hold the pill between your thumb and first finger and drop it as far back in the dog's mouth as possible before closing the jaws. Stroking the underside of the lower jaw should encourage the dog to swallow the pill.
- If it proves impossible to dose your dog in this way, you may be able to disguise the pill by pressing it into a treat.

WHAT IS THE BEST WAY TO APPLY EYE OINTMENT? IT STICKS IN THE TUBE, AND IS HARD TO SQUEEZE OUT.

- Ophthalmic ointments do not need to be refrigerated unless this is specifically indicated on the tube.
- They can be easily applied to the eye of a dog at room temperature.
- Steady your dog's muzzle with one hand, and roll the lower eyelid downward with your thumb to form a pocket.
- The tip of the ointment tube is quite smooth, and will cause no pain or injury if directed into the pouch thus formed.
- Squeeze about a quarter-inch of ointment into the lid-pouch.
- Once there, the ointment will quickly melt and dissipate over the surface of the eye.
- Administer according to label directions.

HOW DO I GIVE LIQUID MEDICINE TO A DOG?

- Draw up the correct dosage of medicine into the syringe.
- Open the dog's mouth as if to administer a pill, and carefully squirt the medicine into the back of the mouth.
- Close the dog's mouth at intervals to encourage it to swallow.
- Don't put in too much at once, or the dog may choke and spit out the liquid.

- There is little doubt that alternative forms of medicine can be of value to dogs, and a number of veterinary practices now offer both the conventional and alternative methods of treatment, including homoeopathy, herbalism, and acupuncture.
- Most health insurance plans for dogs cover the costs of alternative treatments, if recommended by your veterinarian.

CAN DOGS BENEFIT FROM ALTERNATIVE MEDICINE?

first aid

How to deal with a dog in an emergency situation.

- A dog that is lying still in a traffic lane should be covered and moved as soon as possible. This is a job for trained persons, such as the police or animal control officers.
- Since you don't know if the dog is living or dead, don't play hero and become another traffic statistic.
- If it is alive, it should receive immediate veterinary care.
- If dead, it should be moved from the road to prevent being the cause of other traffic accidents.
- Your actions should be limited to assisting in directing traffic from a safe distance after the police have been called.

- A dog that has suffered a car collision and is still on its feet will be panicky at the very least.
- For a novice to attempt to handle such a dog would be foolish. Call the police, and ask them to advise the dog control warden. Don't corner or try to catch the dog involved. If it has been seriously injured, it might become aggressive toward any person who approaches it. The greatest help you can render at such a time will be to try to comfort the dog from several feet away. Above all, watch the traffic!

An injured dog moved to the side of the road to prevent it causing other traffic accidents.

A collapsed dog covered by a coat to comfort it.

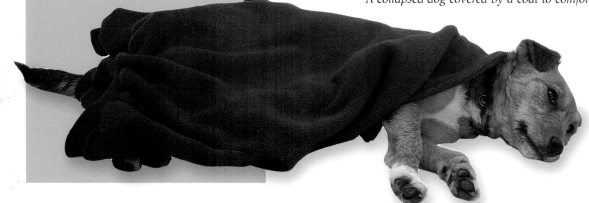

WHAT SHOULD I DO WITH A DOG THAT SURVIVES AN ACCIDENT?

- You must arrange for the dog to be seen by a veterinarian, even if it appears to be relatively unaffected by its experience. Internal hemorrhaging is a risk that if undetected could cause the dog to collapse later. X-rays can be taken if fractures are suspected.
- Superficial injuries, such as friction burns, are also likely to heal more rapidly if cleaned and dressed professionally.
- If the dog is not yours, be aware that there are liabilities involved with taking someone else's dog to a veterinarian for treatment.
- Unless you know the owners of the dog and are willing to risk a lawsuit, the best plan is to call for the appropriate officials who will contact the dog's owner and deliver the dog to an emergency veterinary clinic.

If a dog requires CPR, you must get professional help unless you are trained to administer such aid.

- The pads may appear to be tough, but they will bleed profusely if lacerated.
- Their innervation makes it very painful for the dog to place a wounded foot on the ground. Shards of glass and the lids of cans can cause deep cuts to the foot pads.
- Bind such an injury with a bandage and consult your veterinarian in case it needs suturing.

HOW ROBUST ARE A DOG'S FOOT PADS? CAN THEY BE EASILY INJURED?

- Nails or pieces of wire that become impaled in the pads must also be removed by a veterinarian to minimize pain and the risk of infection.

HOW CAN I KNOW THE DOG IS DEAD? IS THERE ANYTHING THAT I CAN DO TO TRY TO REVIVE IT?

- Call the police or animal control officers. If the dog is alive but comatose, this is a situation for professional help.
- Don't handle the head of a dog that may be alive or you are likely to be bitten.
- If the dog is alive and needs CPR, and you have been trained to administer such aid, you can do so at your own risk.
- You should be able to tell if the dog is dead by checking for a femoral pulse (see page 101).

WHAT ARE THE SYMPTOMS OF HEATSTROKE, AND WHAT SHOULD I DO IF MY DOG DOES SHOW SERIOUS SIGNS OF DISTRESS?

- The dog will breathe with its mouth open and may then start panting rapidly.
- This is a sign that it could shortly collapse from heat exhaustion.
- Act quickly to place your dog in the shade, and provide it with a drink of cold water if possible.
- If the dog collapses, you must try to immerse it in a bath of cool water to dissipate the heat from its body and help it to recover.

WHAT IS FLY STRIKE OR MYIASIS?

- Myiasis is an infestation by the maggots of a fly. It typically occurs in the summertime in temperate parts of the world but is a constant hazard in the tropics.
- Older dogs especially are at risk, as are dogs whose coats have become stained by organic matter as a result of injury or diarrhea.
- Flies are attracted to the contaminated hair, where they lay their eggs. Within a few days the eggs hatch into maggots which bore into the dog's flesh. They feed on the dog's tissue and produce toxins that ultimately enter the dog's circulatory system. These can be fatal, and thus rapid treatment is needed.
- The affected area should be cleaned and the contaminated fur cut away to reveal the damage beneath.
- The maggots must be removed with tweezers, and the wound should be dressed with a suitable insecticidal powder to dry it up and facilitate healing. Antibiotics may also be required.

WHAT SHOULD I DO IF MY DOG IS BITTEN BY A SNAKE WHEN WE ARE OUT FOR A WALK?

- Poisonous snakebites can be fatal. The most important thing is to keep the bitten animal as quiet as possible.
- Pick up the dog, put it in your car, and proceed to the veterinary hospital immediately.
- Don't let the dog walk or run about. If necessary, restrain it with a blanket or your coat. Hold the dog and keep it quiet, and do not cut the fang marks.

WHAT SHOULD I DO IF MY PUPPY IS STUNG BY A WASP OR BEE?

- Until a puppy has experienced the pain of a sting, this remains a risk. A sting on the tongue is especially hazardous, because the tongue will swell rapidly and may make breathing difficult.
- If you witness the incident, try to identify the insect and the site of the sting. It may be possible to extract a bee sting with the aid of tweezers and a magnifying glass, and thus lessen its impact.
- An anti-sting remedy can help, but it may be necessary to seek veterinary assistance.
- Some dogs are allergic to stings, and urgent treatment is then important to prevent a serious adverse reaction.

SHOULD I USE A HEATING PAD TO PROVIDE EXTRA WARMTH FOR MY SICK DOG?

- Extra heat is rarely necessary or advised.
- If your veterinarian suggests additional heat for the comfort of your pet, place the heating pad under several thicknesses of blanket, or under its bed and bedding.
- Be sure that neither the cord nor any electrical connections are exposed.

There are so many unwanted dogs in the world today that breeding should be carried out in a responsible way to avoid exacerbating the problem. Never be prepared to let your bitch have a litter of puppies unless you are willing to feed and look after them for months until you can find good homes for them. While puppies from top show lines will always be in demand, those from mixed- breed parents will almost certainly only appeal to potential owners seeking pets themselves. As a

8 Breeding

result, it will be much better to have your dog neutered at an early stage, partly because this will make your dog or bitch easier to live with. The surgery is relatively safe and straightforward, although it it irreversible.

There are unlikely to be any long-term complications arising from surgery.

basic instincts

Describes signs of your pet's sexual maturity, and advice on breeding.

AT WHAT AGE DO DOGS BECOME SEXUALLY MATURE?

- This depends to some extent on the size and breed of the dog.
- Smaller dogs generally mature before their larger relatives.
- Females may have their first heat at 6 months of age, although 12 months is more likely, and it may be 18 months in the case of one of the giant breeds.
- Males mature at about the same age, although some may be able to breed at an earlier stage. This may be breed-specific; male Beagles, for example, mature earlier than bitches, while in the Chow Chow, the reverse is the case.
- Breeding a male or female less than 2 years old is never advised.

WHAT ARE THE SIGNS OF SEXUAL MATURITY?

- When a female of about 6 months reaches sexual maturity, she will begin the estrous or heat cycle that lasts about three weeks and recurs about every seven to eight months.
- The outward signs that accompany this cycle announce her sexual maturity and ability to reproduce.
- Males show their maturity by beginning to notice the scents of other dogs, and by raising a hind leg when urinating, although this sign is variable.
- They often become more aggressive toward other male dogs and tend to mark their territory with urine.

MY DOG APPEARS TO HAVE ONLY ONE TESTICLE IN HIS SCROTUM. IS THIS SERIOUS?

- The testicles are developed in the abdomen and shortly after birth they descend into the scrotum.
- If only one is present in the scrotum by 3 months of age, the dog is termed a monorchid.
- The retention of a testicle in the abdomen is quite significant. A monorchid dog is not allowed in purebred competitions because the condition is hereditary.
- The retained testicle may become cancerous and should be removed. The normal testicle should also be removed to prevent the condition from being passed to offspring.

A sexually mature dog can mate at any time and will be attracted to any bitch in heat.

ARE MALE DOGS ONLY ABLE TO MATE SEASONALLY AS WELL?

- Male dogs that have attained sexual maturity can mate at any time. Females in heat attract males for miles around if they are outside, and a backyard fence usually doesn't interfere with a persistent male's advances.
- The bulbo-urethral gland of the dog's penis swells during copulation and ties the male and female together. The tie may last for 15 or 20 minutes, and when it occurs, the dogs often turn to face opposite directions.
- You should never try to separate them during this tie. Ejaculation of sperm occurs early in the tie, but fluids that are continually produced are important to the survival of sperm.

HOW WILL I KNOW WHEN OUR BITCH COMES INTO HEAT?

- The initial sign of a female's heat or estrous cycle is a swelling of the vulva, which approximates the beginning of proestrus. It is accompanied by bleeding from the genital tract.
- This bloody discharge changes to a light straw-colored fluid, during which time breeding can occur. This is the estrus period.
- This stage is followed by diestrus, the period that includes pregnancy if the bitch is bred. The anestrus period is the resting stage of the estrous cycle.
- Ovulation is not visible outwardly, but it occurs in the first few days of estrus. Heat lasts for about three weeks and recurs about every seven or eight months.

mating

What to expect when you decide to breed your dog, and the possible pitfalls.

Airedale Terrier stud can be found through breed organizations

- In most cases, you will be expected to pay a stud fee.
- Check what conditions apply if your bitch does not conceive: Will the fee be refunded, or will another mating be provided free of charge?
- Sometimes the owner of the stud dog will waive the stud fee in return for some of the puppies. In this case, it must be absolutely clear how the litter will be shared.

WHAT ARRANGEMENTS SHOULD I MAKE WITH THE OWNER OF THE STUD DOG?

- The terms of any agreement should be in writing and signed by both parties.
- Once your bitch shows signs of proestrus, she will need to be taken to the kennel of the stud dog, so that she can settle in there before mating occurs.
- Remember to take her vaccination certificate with you.

I WANT TO BREED FROM MY BITCH. HOW DO I FIND A STUD DOG?

- First, consider what you plan to do with the puppies. You must be willing to keep them yourself if you cannot find suitable homes for them.
- For show purposes, buy the best bitch you can afford. If you have already shown her, you will have some indication of where her strengths and weaknesses lie.
- Kennels with potentially suitable stud dogs can be contacted through the breed organization, and most breeders will be happy to advise on the best choice.
- They may need to see your bitch, or possibly photographs and a video of her, in advance.

SHOULD I HAVE MY BITCH CHECKED BY A VETERINARIAN BEFORE MATING HER?

- This can be beneficial, not only to confirm her suitability for breeding purposes, but also to make sure that her vaccinations are current.
- The bitch will then be able to transfer some of the protection provided by vaccination to her pups.
- Deworming can also be done if needed to lessen the likelihood of the puppies acquiring roundworms from their mother.

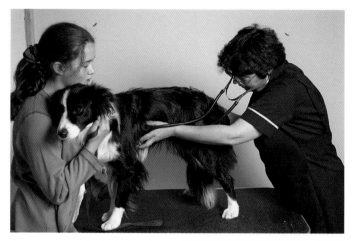

A veterinarian will check that the bitch's vaccinations are current.

- This can happen. A bitch in heat will be prepared to mate with more than one dog, which is why it is important to keep her isolated from other males after mating, until her estrus period has passed.

HOW DO I PREVENT MY BITCH GIVING BIRTH TO A LITTER CONTAINING PUPS SIRED BY TWO DIFFERENT MALE DOGS?

To ensure the litter is sired by one male, keep a bitch in heat isolated from other males initially.

- In fact, it is normal practice for a bitch to be mated twice during this period to assure maximum fertility.
- If mating occurs just before ovulation, sperm are likely to be present in the reproductive tract, but a subsequent mating will boost their number.

- It is usually possible for a veterinarian to determine whether a bitch is pregnant three weeks to a month after mating, by careful palpation of the abdominal area.
- An ultrasonic scan may reveal the presence of puppies at a slightly earlier stage.
- If the outcome is negative, your bitch will simply enter the diestrus period and come back into heat again in due course.
- Most bitches come into heat twice a year, but a few breeds, such as the Basenji and Tibetan Mastiff may only have one period of heat annually.
- The interval between heats can vary in individual dogs, however, from as long as eight months to as short as two.
- If repeated mating fails to yield the desired result, a veterinary investigation is advisable.

WHAT HAPPENS IF THE MATING PROVES UNSUCCESSFUL?

IS MY DOG AT ANY RISK OF CATCHING A SEXUALLY TRANSMITTED DISEASE AS THE RESULT OF MATING?

- There are a number of sexually transmitted diseases of the dog.
- Canine herpes virus is host-specific for the dog and can cause lack of conception or abortion.
- Brucellosis, the serious chronic and permanent genital infection of both males and females, is transmitted sexually.
- Treatments are futile, and once brucellosis has infected an animal, it is sterile for life. Canine venereal tumors are also contracted by breeding.
- They are found in and around the genitalia and in some cases around the mouth and elsewhere.

pregnancy

How to recognize the signs of pregnancy,

and the changes that take place in your bitch.

HOW SOON IS MY BITCH LIKELY TO SHOW OBVIOUS SIGNS OF PREGNANCY?

- External signs may not be apparent until the fifth week of pregnancy.
- The abdomen will start to enlarge, and the nipples will swell and become pinker, reflecting the increased blood flow to this part of the body as the time for birth approaches.
- Avoid handling your bitch more than necessary, and don't feel her abdomen, because this could be harmful.

HOW DO THE UNBORN PUPPIES DEVELOP?

- In the period immediately after mating, the fertilized egg develops into an expanding mass of cells known as the zygote.
- By nineteen days this implants into the wall of the uterus, where the placental connection will develop to nourish and sustain the embryo over the nine weeks of the pregnancy.
- The uterus of the female dog comprises two sections, known as horns, which can accommodate many embryos, and bitches rarely produce just one offspring.
- Organogenesis (the development of the body organs) is usually complete by the time the fetuses are 5 weeks old, after which the major growth spurt takes place.

A full-term pregnant Corgi bitch lying down.

Your dog is unlikely to require any basic change in her diet until the final trimester, when the unborn puppies begin to grow bigger.

WILL SHE NEED A SPECIAL DIET?

For the last six weeks of the pregnancy, increase the bitch's food allowance by about 10 percent.

Before then, the puppies do not make major nutritional demands on the mother's bodily resources; the puppies of a typical 30-pound Beagle, for example, will only weigh approximately ½ oz. each, six weeks after mating has occurred.

It is important not to overfeed the bitch in the early stages of pregnancy, because obesity may make delivery more difficult.

Increase her food allowance by about 10 percent from six weeks to the end of the pregnancy. Offer three or four smaller meals a day, because the growing fetuses will press on her stomach and reduce its capacity.

Supplements, such as calcium in particular, may be needed and should be discussed with your veterinarian.

IS IT SAFE TO EXERCISE HER NORMALLY DURING PREGNANCY?

Regular periods of exercise are important throughout the early weeks of pregnancy to maintain the bitch's muscle tone and general fitness.

Once the fetuses start growing, and she begins to put on weight, however, allow her to dictate the pace and distance that you walk each day. Several shorter walks will be preferable to one longer hike.

The weight gain in the latter part of pregnancy can be 15 pounds or more, so at this stage, your bitch's enthusiasm for exercise is likely to decline noticeably.

Don't encourage her to jump up toward the end of her pregnancy.

Regular periods of exercise are important for a pregnant dog, but do not encourage her to jump up.

birth

Although most births proceed without any problems, it is useful to know the normal sequence of events and when to contact the veterinarian for advice.

Border Collie
suckling
her pups.

HOW MANY PUPPIES ARE LIKELY TO BE BORN?

- This depends partly on the individual and also on the breed. A young dog having her first litter is likely to have fewer puppies, similarly an older individual will probably also have a small litter.
- The majority of litters comprise four to seven puppies. The smallest breeds tend to have the fewest puppies per litter, but there are exceptions. Pekingese, for example, may have as many as ten puppies.
- The largest litter of Pekingese on record consisted of twenty-three puppies!

WHAT PREPARATIONS SHOULD I MAKE FOR THE BIRTH?

- You must provide a whelping box in a quiet part of your home, where the bitch can give birth.
- The box need not be of elaborate construction, but it must have low sides to give the bitch easy access, and be wide enough to enable her to stretch out comfortably.
- It is important to include a simple anti-crush bar to prevent any of the puppies from being inadvertently squashed by their mother. Line the whelping box with newspaper covered by an old clean towel.
- Protect the floor, if necessary, with a layer of plastic and some newspaper. Accustom the bitch to sleeping in the box, so that she will automatically use it when the puppies are due.

Yellow Labrador
Retriever poses with
her 6-week-old
puppies.

- It is normal for your bitch to appear distressed, especially at first. She is likely to pant and to shiver at intervals, up to a day before giving birth, although this first stage of labor generally passes more quickly. Observe her discreetly at this stage. In due course, the puppies will begin to emerge, usually headfirst, in rapid succession.
- Often they are still covered in the amniotic sac that encased them during pregnancy.

WHAT IS THE NORMAL SEQUENCE OF EVENTS DURING BIRTH?

- The dam will break away this covering, and lick each puppy vigorously to encourage it to start breathing.
- The placenta is passed about 15 minutes after the birth of each puppy, and may be eaten by the dam. Check that there is a placenta for each puppy, because the retention of a placenta in the bitch's body can lead to serious infection.
- It normally takes about six hours for the puppies in a litter to be born.

WHAT ARE THE EARLIEST INDICATORS THAT THE BIRTH IS IMMINENT?

- Pregnancy typically lasts about sixty-three days. The first obvious signs that the birth is imminent are restlessness and obvious loss of appetite.
- Body temperature drops to 99.5°F. The vulva enlarges, and the pelvic ligaments slacken in preparation for the birth, so that the bony prominences at the top of the pelvis are more pronounced.

The bitch in labor with her fourth puppy.

The bitch frees the new-born puppy from the fetal membranes.

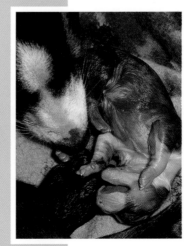

The newborn puppy takes its first breath.

Four-day-old Border Collie puppies suckling.

● There are several common whelping problems that can happen. Most puppies are born headfirst, but it is normal for posterior presentations to occur. A breech birth is when a puppy's tail and rear end face into the birth canal, with the hind legs folded forward. Sometimes the bitch is small and immature and the bones of her pelvis won't allow the passage of puppies. In case of large litters, the bitch's uterine muscle fatigues and delivery ceases. In some breeds, such as the Bulldog, deformities of puppies may interfere with delivery. In cases of dystocia, or difficult birth, call your veterinarian for advice.

WHAT PROBLEMS MAY BE ENCOUNTERED WITH BREECH BIRTHS?

ARE SOME BREEDS MORE PRONE TO BIRTH PROBLEMS THAN OTHERS?

● The puppies of breeds that have large heads relative to their bodies, such as Bulldogs, are at greater risk of becoming lodged in the birth canal.
● Under these circumstances, it may be necessary for a veterinarian to carry out a cesarean section. Always seek advice from your veterinarian if you are concerned about the progress of any delivery.

The relatively large heads of breeds such as Bulldogs, Bullmastiffs, and Staffordshire Bull Terriers can cause problems at birth.

Bulldog

Bullmastiff

Staffordshire Bull Terrier

bitch & new puppies

Feeding your dog at this stage, weaning the puppies, and checking for problems.

- After the birth, the bitch will be tired. She will probably want a drink rather than food. She will then rest with her puppies, then start suckling. This is vital, because colostrum, the first fluid from the mammary glands, contains antibodies to protect them from infection until their own immune systems become functional.
- Check that all the puppies are suckling and place weaker individuals in contact with a teat. The puppies will feed every two hours.
- Keep the room temperature at 70°F, because the puppies cannot yet regulate their own temperature.

The puppies will not make any noises unless they have a problem, such as a shortage of food or a cold environment.

WHAT PROBLEMS COULD ARISE DURING THE WEANING PERIOD?

- Mastitis is an infection of one or more of the dam's mammary glands, which causes swelling and often discoloration of the affected area. The pain will make it impossible for her to suckle her puppies normally, and hand-feeding will be necessary. Antibiotic therapy is usually required.
- Another problem that can arise is eclampsia—also known as milk fever. This results from a shortage of available calcium. It occurs most in small dogs that have large litters.
- Milk fever happens when the puppies are 2–4 weeks old and the demand for milk is highest. Symptoms of milk fever are unsteadiness and disorientation, followed by convulsions and collapse.
- Seek treatment quickly, when the injection of a suitable calcium compound can produce rapid recovery.

HOW COULD I HAND-REAR THE PUPPIES IF NECESSARY?

- Milk replacers are formulated to match the constituents of bitch's milk, but they do not contain the protective immunoglobulins. It is therefore important to allow puppies to suckle at first, even if you must then rear some or all of them by hand.
- Some protection against infection can subsequently be provided by adding a probiotic product (see page 60) to the milk. The food must be freshly mixed for each feed, and the feeding tools must be thoroughly cleaned and disinfected between meals.
- Wipe the fur around the puppy's lips after each meal. Your veterinarian will show you how to feed the puppies most effectively.

AT WHAT AGE SHOULD THE PUPPIES BE GIVEN SOLID FOOD AND HOW SHOULD WEANING BE DONE?

- Start to offer the pups a little canned puppy food when they are about 3–4 weeks old.
- Keep it out of reach of the dam, because she will eat it before they can. Place the food on a saucer but hold a morsel up to their noses so that they can sample it directly first.
- Within two or three weeks, the puppies should eat happily on their own. Offer them four meals a day at first. The first and last meals should consist of a milk-replacer food.
- The actual amount of food will depend largely on the size of the puppies. Consult your veterinarian if in doubt (see page 49).

HOW MUCH FOOD SHOULD I OFFER TO A BITCH WITH PUPPIES?

- The dam's food intake must increase greatly to meet the rapid growth needs of her puppies. Provide 50 percent more than her usual intake in the first week, and double that amount at the start of the second week. By the time the puppies are 3 weeks old, the dam should be receiving three times her regular ration, supplied in three or four meals through the day.
- Her fluid intake will also rise dramatically to maintain her output of milk.
- Provide a bowl of fresh water with every feed, and keep a continuous supply of drinking water available.

HOW WILL THE BITCH INDICATE THAT THE PUPPIES ARE BEING WEANED?

- The puppies' reduced demand for milk goes hand in hand with a decreased supply from the dam.
- The emergence of the deciduous or milk teeth by the time a puppy is 6 weeks old is likely to increase her reluctance to allow the pups to suckle.
- At first, she may vomit food for the puppies. This is natural behavior, and the partially digested food is readily consumed by the young pups.

By the time puppies are 6 weeks old, their deciduous or milk teeth should have appeared and they should be able to manage solid food (above). The bitch will then avoid suckling her puppies, as the Border Collie shows by leaping over them (top).

pregnancy prevention

Preventing unwanted pregnancy by isolating, spaying or neutering your dog.

- Keep her indoors, allowing her outside for exercise only with strict supervision. Ordinarily, injections or tablets to prevent estrus are not advisable.
- Kenneling her in a boarding facility is an option.
- Spaying the dog is the best permanent method of preventing estrus and inadvertent breeding. This also prevents subsequent serious conditions, such as pyometra and mammary tumors.

IS IT DANGEROUS FOR BITCHES TO BREED LATE IN LIFE? DOES THEIR FERTILITY DECLINE?

- Bitches that are not spayed will continue to have periods of heat, although these may become less frequent as the dog becomes older.
- There is an increased risk of complications with pregnancy in an older animal.
- Spaying is recommended when a bitch's active reproductive life is over.

WILL A MALE DOG STILL RETAIN THE URGE TO MATE AFTER BEING NEUTERED?

- If the dog mated regularly before being neutered, the urge to mate is likely to continue until the level of testosterone in his body subsides, at which point his desire to mate will also decline.
- Neutering helps to alter the behavior of a male dog that seeks relief by mounting a person's leg.

Understanding your dog is a vital part of ownership. You will then be able to recognize when there is a problem affecting your pet and trained behavior counselors can help in cases of behavioral problems affecting your dog. Those dogs that have been rescued from bad homes are most likely to have behavioral problems.

9 Behavior

These manifest themselves in many ways, from dislike of a particular garment to an irresistible desire to eat excrement. Other problems that can occur are specific to a certain breed of dog. A study of the pedigrees of affected dogs usually shows a common ancestry. The behavior can range from a mild snapping in the air, to a much more alarming rage syndrome that is regarded as a form of epilepsy. Other obvious behavioral problems, such as urination in the home, may have an underlying medical cause, which is why it is important to discuss these matters with your veterinarian as a first course of action.

dog's life

Understanding the way your dog perceives the world about it, and why it behaves in certain ways.

DO DOGS SEE THE SAME IMAGE OF THE WORLD AS WE DO?

- The eyes of dogs are positioned closer to the sides of the face than human eyes are, and this gives them a broader field of vision than ours.
- Generally speaking, dogs can see about three-quarters of the way around them, whereas human eyes detect an image equivalent to a half-circle.

- Broad-headed dogs have a better field of vision than their arrow-headed counterparts. Humans have better overlap of vision in the central area (binocular vision), which means that we can discern a sharper image, whereas dogs detect moving images, even in the distance, more readily.

WHY IS DEAFNESS ASSOCIATED WITH WHITE DOGS?

- The ear canals of all puppies open by three weeks of age. In some dogs, however, the inner ear is deformed by a genetic weakness that is linked to coat color, and such dogs are deaf.
- The problem is most marked in white Boxers, Bull Terriers, Sealyham Terriers, and Dalmatians.
- Deafness can be difficult to identify with certainty, because a noise, such as clapping your hands close to your dog, creates soundwaves that it will detect.
- The relative absence of movement of the ears can be an indication of deafness. If your puppy is very slow to respond to its name, and appears generally unresponsive, you should consult your veterinarian.

DO DOGS SEE IN COLOR?

- Two types of cells are present on the retina at the back of the eye, where the image is formed.
- Rods provide the ability to see in relatively poor light, whereas cones, which are stimulated by bright light, are required for effective color vision.
- Dogs have a much higher ratio of rods to cones than we do, which means that they can see in conditions that appear completely dark to us, but conversely, they cannot see as well as we do in color.

- Dogs curl up to conserve their body heat, and possibly they also feel more secure when sleeping in this position.
- Many wild dogs seek out caves and rocky outcrops as sleeping places and must often curl up to fit into a small area.
- As the dog becomes more relaxed, it will stretch out on its side, if space allows, especially in a hot environment.

WHY DOES A DOG CURL IN A BALL AT FIRST WHEN IT SLEEPS AND THEN STRETCH OUT?

DO DOGS DREAM?

- Dogs undergo periods of REM (rapid eye movement) sleep similar to those that denote the occurrence of dreaming in humans, so it seems highly probable that dogs do dream.
- During REM sleep, they may also twitch, and their legs may move. REM sleep occurs within half an hour of the dog's falling asleep and recurs at intervals.
- Young puppies, however, appear to dream more, because they experience only REM sleep in their early months.

WHY DOES MY DOG DIG IN THE FLOWER BED AND TRY TO BURY ITS BONE HERE?

- This is an echo of the behavior of the dog's ancestor, the wolf. Packs of wolves often overpower quarry larger than themselves. Food is precious, and if they cannot eat all the meat on the carcass, they bury what remains to conceal it from scavengers and keep it available to the pack over several days.
- Similarly, your dog has sufficient food and does not require its bone immediately. In due course, the dog will return and excavate the bone.
- This is not recommended, however, because any flesh on the bone will have started to decay, and may disturb your dog's digestion.
- It is better to provide an artificial chew, which is less likely to be buried.

DO GREYHOUNDS JUMP IN THE AIR AS THEY RUN AROUND THE TRACK?

- Sequences of photographs, pioneered by those of Edward Muybridge in 1887, reveal that Greyhounds take all their feet off the track as part of their normal running action.
- The movement begins when the muscular hind legs push the dog forward into a leap; after landing, it bounds upward again, using its front legs to provide the propulsive thrust.
- At this point, the hind legs come forward and the front legs simultaneously go backward, so that both pairs are clear of the ground.

WHY DOES MY DOG SCRATCH AT THE GROUND AFTER URINATING?

- This is a territorial marker, providing visual evidence of your dog's recent presence to other dogs that pass the spot. The scratching reinforces the scent of the urine and may also deposit traces of scent from between the toe pads as an additional means of identification to another dog.

WHY DOES MY DOG DRAG HIS HINDQUARTERS ALONG THE GROUND? IS THIS A SIGN OF IMPENDING PARALYSIS?

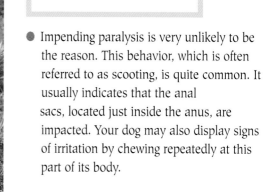

- Impending paralysis is very unlikely to be the reason. This behavior, which is often referred to as scooting, is quite common. It usually indicates that the anal sacs, located just inside the anus, are impacted. Your dog may also display signs of irritation by chewing repeatedly at this part of its body.

- This behavior is most often seen in puppies that have recently been separated from their littermates, and probably reflects the puppy's earlier play with its companions.
- The pup may not immediately identify the tail as its own. The behavior is soon abandoned as the puppy grows, and it is harmless, provided that the puppy shows no sign of discomfort.
- Playing with the puppy will distract it from behaving this way.

WHY DO PUPPIES CHASE THEIR TAILS?

- This is another ancestral characteristic. Having made a kill, wolves are vulnerable to other predators. They therefore eat as much and as quickly as they can.
- The shape of their teeth shows that dogs are not equipped to grind food, but to tear it into chunks for swallowing.
- If your dog stops gulping its food, and appears to eat reluctantly, it may have a dental problem.

WHY DOES MY DOG ALWAYS GULP HIS FOOD DOWN, RATHER THAN CHEWING IT? IT SEEMS AS IF HE IS STARVING, BUT THIS ISN'T THE CASE!

Don't examine your dog's mouth, which is likely to be tender. Your veterinarian will carry out a proper investigation of the cause, and can sedate your pet if necessary.

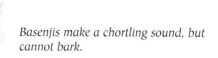

Basenjis make a chortling sound, but cannot bark.

WHY DON'T BASENJIS BARK LIKE OTHER DOGS?

- The Basenji is one of the few breeds to originate from Africa, where it was kept as a hunting dog for many years before becoming known elsewhere.
- The larynx of these dogs is structured in such a way that their vocal cords cannot vibrate as strongly as those of other breeds.
- As a result, they make chortling sounds but cannot bark.
- This anatomical peculiarity causes no problem for the dogs.

WHY DO DOGS ROLL ON THE GROUND?

- There appears to be no particular reason.
- When dogs do this, they are usually relaxed, and it is probably simply a way of stretching and toning the muscles in the back.
- This action should not be confused with submissive behavior in which a dog rolls over to show that it presents no challenge to a rival, and usually defuses conflict as a result.

HOW DO DOGS FOLLOW TRAILS SO ACCURATELY?

- Smell is the dog's most powerful sense. It is so highly developed that dogs can identify and respond to the minutest trace of scent, even when it emanates from a buried object.
- If a dog has eaten, however, its trailing ability is reduced, especially if it has consumed any fat.
- Conversely, a hungry dog follows a trail more effectively.

The Bloodhound has the keenest sense of smell of any domestic animal.

WHAT DOES MY DOG USE ITS WHISKERS FOR?

- The whiskers, or vibrissae, are specialized hairs, which are thicker than normal hairs and have a sensory function.
- They are arranged in tufts, with those running along each side of the muzzle being the most prominent. The latter may help the dog to judge whether an opening is wide enough for it to slip through.
- The whiskers on the underside of the jaw, known as the intra-ramal group, indicate the position of the jaw relative to the ground.
- The whiskers above the eyes probably have a protective function, alerting the dog to the closeness of a potential hazard in its environment before it touches the eye.

A dog's whiskers perform a sensory function and can help the dog judge the width of an opening.

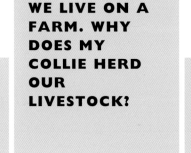

WHY ARE DOGS ATTRACTED TO ANISE?

● They may not be. Research with day-old puppies showed that they did not find the scent of anise instinctively appealing.

● The pungent oil from the seeds of the anise plant has traditionally been exploited for its power to mask other smells. Criminals used anise to put tracker dogs literally off the scent.

● Anise is also used to lay trails for drag-hunting purposes, and it is now thought that dogs follow this scent simply because of conditioning, because at the end of the trail, they are likely to be rewarded.

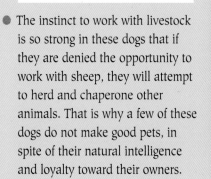

WE LIVE ON A FARM. WHY DOES MY COLLIE HERD OUR LIVESTOCK?

● The instinct to work with livestock is so strong in these dogs that if they are denied the opportunity to work with sheep, they will attempt to herd and chaperone other animals. That is why a few of these dogs do not make good pets, in spite of their natural intelligence and loyalty toward their owners.

WHY IS MY BITCH PRODUCING MILK FROM HER MAMMARY GLANDS, ALTHOUGH SHE HAS NO PUPPIES?

- This is an indication of a false pregnancy. Under normal circumstances, when ovulation occurs, structures known as corpora lutea develop at the sites where the ova were released.
- They produce the hormone progesterone, which helps to maintain the pregnancy at this critical early stage.
- If mating does not occur, the corpora lutea normally regress. In the case of a false pregnancy, this does not happen, so that the output of progesterone continues, and it stimulates the output of milk.

Border Collie bitch suffering from a false pregnancy with a soft toy and two of her daughter's four-day-old puppies to mother.

HOW SHOULD I TREAT A FALSE PREGNANCY?

- The milk will soon dry up, but the problem is likely to recur after your bitch's next heat.
- Allowing her to breed at her next heat will not eliminate the risk of recurrence.
- There is some evidence that bitches that suffer regular false pregnancies may be more susceptible to pyometra (infection of the womb) later in their lives.
- The recommended solution, therefore, is to have your bitch spayed once the signs of the false pregnancy have subsided.
- If you want to allow her to have a litter first, let her breed at the earliest possible occasion.

communication

Describes the way in which your dog communicates with you and with other animals.

WHY DOES MY DOG STOP AT EVERY LAMPPOST AND LIFT HIS LEG?

- This is the typical behavior of a male dog and serves as a territorial indicator. In addition to removing waste products from the body, a dog's urine acts as a means of communication.
- Its scent identifies the individual, and dogs sniff repeatedly at sites where urine is deposited to gain clues to the other dogs that have used that route recently.
- Dogs that are taken on the same walk every day tend to urinate at particular spots, reinforcing the scent that they leave there.

- This trait is linked with the onset of puberty and is triggered by the hormone testosterone, which is responsible for much of the male dog's sexual behavior.
- If a young male is neutered before puberty, it will continue to urinate by squatting for the remainder of its life.
- Female dogs have a relatively low level of testosterone and normally squat when urinating. The ability to raise either of their hind legs enables mature male dogs to mark their scent more effectively, and they target areas such as trees that will not be missed by other dogs.

WHY DO MALE DOGS URINATE OVER VERTICAL OBJECTS, SUCH AS TREES, WHILE BITCHES AND PUPPIES OF BOTH SEXES SQUAT?

DO DOGS UNDERSTAND WHAT THEIR OWNERS SAY?

- Although the bond between owner and dog can be very strong, a dog does not comprehend the meaning of your words as such.
- It interprets the sounds of your commands and thus comes to recognize what is required of it, and even sometimes to pre-empt your instructions.
- This is especially likely in breeds that are used to working closely with people.
- Communication between dog and owner is not exclusively verbal, since hand signals are also used to convey instructions to the dog, often from a long distance away.

IS IT DANGEROUS FOR DOGS TO SNIFF AT LAMPPOSTS?

Bichon Frisé have squat, compact body shapes and can easily maintain their balance when begging.

- There is a risk associated with such behavior, especially in urban areas where dog populations are denser and there may be a contingent of unvaccinated stray dogs, as well as foxes. A number of diseases can be spread through urine, notably canine adenovirus type 1.
- The urine of an infected dog remains a hazard for up to six months after its recovery, and the virus can survive in the environment for months.
- Leptospirosis is also present in the urine of infected dogs. Keeping your dog's vaccinations current can, however, protect it from both these diseases.

WHY HAS MY DOG STARTED TO BEG?

- Some breeds have a highly playful side to thier natures, which has led to their employment as entertainers in circuses and on sidewalks for centuries.
- The Bichon Frisé is a typical example. They can learn tricks very rapidly.
- Dogs that have a fairly squat, compact body shape find it easiest to beg, because they can maintain their balance more easily.
- Once they realize that this is likely to bring a reward, they will repeat the behavior.

WHY DOES MY DOG SCRATCH AT THE DOOR TO BE LET BACK INTO THE HOUSE?

- You have unintentionally conditioned your dog to behave this way.
- At first, your dog probably used its paw to try and open the door. But its scratching attracted your attention.
- You then hurried to let your pet in and avoid damage to the door from its claws.
- After this happened a number of times, your dog got the idea that this was the way to gain access to the house.
- This situation is best anticipated when the dog is a puppy. Let the pup out, and call it back after a few minutes, before it asks to come in.

WHAT IS THE PURPOSE OF THE ANAL SACS?

- Dogs use the scent in their feces as well as in their urine to indicate their presence, and the main function of the anal sacs is to transfer the dog's individual scent to its feces.
- The sacs can become blocked, and will then need to be emptied by your veterinarian.
- Repeated blockages are common. Anesthetizing the dog and washing the glands out with saline solution may help to prevent a recurrence.
- If left blocked, a sac may abscess and open channels may develop directly to the outside. These can be slow to heal, as well as being very painful for the dog. As a last resort, it may be necessary to remove the sacs surgically.

DO DOGS USE THEIR TAILS FOR COMMUNICATION PURPOSES?

- A dog relies to a great extent on its tail to communicate its mood.
- A raised tail indicates alertness, and possibly a challenge, depending on the positioning of the ears.
- If the dog's tail is held low, between its legs, this is a gesture of submission.

WHAT IS A PLAY BOW? HOW DO I RECOGNIZE THIS?

- This behavior is most often seen in young dogs and indicates a desire to play, as its name suggests.
- The dog bends down on its front legs, rests them on the ground, and then bounces up and darts a short distance away.
- It can occur when the dog wants a toy thrown for it to chase but feels it is being ignored.
- Play bowing is also common in dogs that live with older people.

- Some breeds such as the German Shepherd still have erect ears, like wolves, but in many hound breeds, the ears are long and hang down over the ear canal. This is thought to protect the more sensitive inner part of the ear from damage.

- It is possible for German Shepherd Dogs to have floppy ears —their puppies are born with ears of this type–but by about six months old, these will have become raised in almost all cases.

- The importance of the ears for communication is most marked in those breeds with floppy ears. An adult dog that is confident will keep its ears in a forward position, but a dog which is under threat from a dominant rival will draw back its ears tightly against the side of the head.

- This provides a visual clue to its opponent that it is not mounting any challenge, while at the same time greater protection is given to its ears if the other dog attacks.

A confident adult dog will keep its ears in a forward position. A dog that feels threatened will draw back its ears as shown by this Ibizan Hound.

behavior modification

How to encourage your dog to modify or stop any

antisocial or dangerous behavior.

WHY DOES MY DOG INSIST ON DRINKING OUT OF THE TOILET?

- This behavior may begin accidentally, but it can quickly become a habit, which must be discouraged.
- Bleach in the water is a hazard to your dog, in addition to the risk of infections.
- The simplest solution is to exclude the dog from the bathroom, and as an added precaution, to keep the toilet lid firmly closed.

HOW DO I ENCOURAGE MY DOG TO DRINK FROM ITS WATER BOWL, RATHER THAN THE GARDEN POND? IS THIS LIKELY TO BE HARMFUL?

- Given the choice, many dogs seem to prefer to drink from standing areas of water, such as ponds or puddles, rather than a clean bowl.
- The reason is unclear. It may be instinctive, or dogs may find drinking more comfortable without the restricting edges of the bowl.
- Dogs should be provided with relatively large drinking bowls with shallow sides unless they have long ears.
- Dogs may simply prefer the taste of standing water, which is softer in some areas than the water from the faucet, in addition to being free from chlorine and similar chemicals.
- Although clean water that is regularly renewed is likely to be safer for them, dogs do not generally suffer illness from drinking out of ponds and similar stretches of water, although there are potential hazards.
- The main risk is from the Leptospira bacterium that is transmitted via rats' urine (see page 109), and dogs should always be vaccinated against leptospirosis.

CAN NEUTERING AFFECT THE BEHAVIOR OF A DOG?

- Neutering can decrease the level of aggression in a male dog, and can make him less likely to roam.
- A spayed bitch will not display the typical signs of heat, and will not be at risk from false pregnancies.
- The effects depend to some extent upon the age at which neutering occurs. Behavioral changes in male dogs are less marked if the dog is already mature.
- If a female is neutered before her first heat, the risk of her subsequently developing mammary tumors is greatly decreased—by up to 200 percent according to some research.

WHY HAS MY DOG STARTED TO CHASE AFTER MOUNTAIN BIKERS WHEN WE ARE OUT WALKING?

- Your dog probably sees this as a game, but it is obviously a potential danger for the riders.
- One solution might be to alter your itinerary in the hope of avoiding them.
- Alternatively, keep your dog on a leash for a few weeks when in the area where the bikers are most likely to be encountered, and scold the dog if it tries to chase after them.
- It is important to keep your dog under control to prevent injury and because you could be liable in case of an accident.
- Check that such an eventuality is covered by your canine or household insurance.

OUR DOG KEEPS ON STEALING FOOD. WHY IS THIS?

- Dogs are scavengers by nature and will rarely resist the opportunity to purloin edible items when their owner's back is turned. Some breeds, including dogs originally bred as pack hounds, have a particularly powerful instinct in this regard.
- The only solution is to keep food out of your dog's reach.
- In the case of giant breeds, such as the Irish Wolfhound, you may need to exclude the dog totally from the kitchen.
- Don't leave garbage in plastic bags that your dog could rip apart. Place them in a secure can with a lid.
- Don't withhold food to punish your dog for its misdemeanor. That may encourage it to scavenge elsewhere.

HOW CAN I KEEP MY DOG FROM SNORING AND DRIBBLING?

- This can prove difficult, especially since some breeds are naturally prone to dribbling, possibly because their lower lips are ill-equipped to retain saliva in their mouths.
- Dribbling is most common in hot weather. The output of saliva increases after eating.
- Short-nosed breeds are most susceptible to snuffling and snoring. This is related to the structure of their faces, although obesity is often a contributory factor.
- Check your dog's diet and its bed, which may be uncomfortable.

fear & aggression

Why your dog behaves in an aggressive,
nervous or frightened manner.

OUR DOG IS VERY FRIGHTENED BY FIREWORKS. CAN I DO ANYTHING TO PREVENT HER FROM BECOMING DISTRESSED?

- Try to anticipate when celebrations featuring fireworks are likely to occur in your neighborhood.
- Take your dog for a good walk just before it becomes dark and then keep her indoors, with the drapes closed to mask the flashes and muffle the sounds of the fireworks.
- Leaving the radio or television on in the room can also help to disguise the noise.
- Following her walk, your dog should be in the mood to sleep. In extreme situations, if all else fails, your veterinarian may prescribe mild tranquilizers.

If another dog attacks your dog try to separate them quickly, to prevent injury.

MY DOG IS NERVOUS BY NATURE. WHAT SHOULD I DO IF IT IS ATTACKED BY A LARGER DOG WHEN WE ARE OUT WALKING?

- You must separate the dogs as quickly as possible to minimize the risk of injury.
- A walking stick will help you fend off the aggressive dog, while you drag your pet off a short distance by its collar. Be aware that your dog will be upset and may attempt to bite.
- Put it back on the leash, and check for signs of injury.
- Discuss the incident with the other owner, from whom you may wish to claim the cost of any ensuing veterinary fees.
- If the person is uncooperative, you might want to report as many details as possible to the police or animal control officer.

An energetic walk will help your dog sleep through the fireworks.

OUR DOG HAS STARTED TO BECOME VERY AGGRESSIVE TOWARD PASSERSBY WHEN WE'RE IN THE CAR. HOW CAN I STOP THIS?

- Some dogs, especially breeds that are protective by nature, exhibit territorial behavior in vehicles and may bark loudly if disturbed there.
- A dog that has experienced teasing while sitting in the car may also develop this problem.
- Effective solutions are not easy, but it is important not to leave your dog alone in the car and to keep it adequately restrained during the journey.

- Although dogs react mainly to scent, they also respond to visual and aural stimuli in their vicinity, particularly after dark.
- Unlike its wolf ancestor, the domestic dog has been encouraged to bark to alert its owner to possible danger. As a result, some dogs bark whenever they detect something out of the ordinary. A puppy may bark because it has not encountered shadows before. In this case, given time, and reassurance if the puppy is nervous, this behavior will cease.

WHY DOES MY DOG BARK AT SHADOWS?

WHY DO DOGS RAISE THEIR HACKLES?

- Raising the hair on the back of the neck can give the dog greater physical presence and make it look more intimidating.
- Dogs often raise their hackles as a warning gesture, when they meet a strange dog or are perturbed by a sudden sound.

DOES GROWLING INDICATE THAT MY DOG WILL BITE?

- Dogs usually display a series of coded signals to each other, based on their body language, rather than suddenly launching into a fight.
- The intention is to make the weaker individual back down before fighting takes place.
- Since the aim is intimidation, the dogs raise themselves to look as large as possible and are likely to growl menacingly.
- As the situation intensifies and fighting becomes imminent, they will bare their teeth.

HOW WILL I KNOW IF MY DOG IS GOING TO FIGHT?

- It is a warning gesture, but it does not necessarily mean that your dog will bite.
- Much depends on the cause.
- Your dog may sense danger rather than directing its growl at a target, as it does in a confrontation with another dog.

WHEN DOGS FIGHT, WILL THEY INJURE EACH OTHER BADLY?

- In most conflicts between two dogs, there is little likelihood of serious injury.
- The dominant individual may snap at its rival, but fights are generally brief, and the loser beats its retreat without delay.
- It may be pursued a short way by the other dog, as an additional assertion of dominance, but the confrontation will end there.

As the puppy approaches the bone, the dominant dog lunges forward with teeth bared.

- This is essential because they were bred to act as guardians, or to fight other dogs.
- In spite of intensive subsequent breeding aimed at raising their threshold of aggression, some of these breeds may still display an adverse reaction to other dogs because of their fighting ancestry.
- Such dogs can attack others with considerable determination and must be kept firmly under control.

WHY ARE SOME DOGS MUCH MORE AGGRESSIVE THAN OTHERS?

In most conflicts, there is little likelihood of serious injury.

social problems

How to assess if antisocial behavior is a medical or a behavioral problem.

MY DOG HAS SUDDENLY STARTED HAVING ACCIDENTS AROUND THE HOME. WHY?

- A medical or behavioral problem could be the cause. Medical conditions may include urinary infections and kidney infections or failure.
- These diseases will often be brought to the owner's attention by the increased consumption of water. Senility, or old age, often is accompanied by defecation or urination in odd places. Behavioral situations, such as jealousy of a new pet in the house, may cause your dog to empty its bowels or bladder in inappropriate places.
- A veterinary examination of the dog should rule out medical problems. Behavioral attitudes can usually be worked out by analyzing what is causing the aberrant behavior and dealing with that.
- If the cause is another pet, pay more attention to the problem dog and see if the behavior stops

CAN DOGS BECOME JEALOUS?

- Jealousy may arise when a new person or pet is introduced into the household. This emotion on the part of the dog is particularly evident when a dog finds its best friend neglecting it in favor of a newborn child, a new wife or husband husband, or in some cases, another pet.
- The dog's behavior may be to act depressed and sullen, or in a few cases, aggressive.
- To prevent or treat jealousy, make an effort to spend a bit more time petting or playing with the dog.
- Take the dog for walks; call it to you for a treat when it least expects it. The result will be acceptance of the new addition to your family and a happier dog.

HOW SHOULD I STOP MY DOG FROM BARKING WHEN I GO OUT, EVEN FOR A SHORT TIME?

- In the case of an elderly dog, it is possible that a deterioration of its hearing or vision is causing it to become disoriented when left alone.
- More often, however this problem is caused by separation anxiety, possibly as a result of the dog being left alone for long periods early in its life. To treat the problem, begin a program of leaving the dog on its own for brief periods only.
- Adopt your usual routine for going out but return after five or ten minutes.
- Praise your dog if has not barked during this period, but do not scold it if it has. Follow this procedure for several weeks, increasing the length of your absences and always taking care to reassure your dog that it is not being abandoned.
- A shock collar that is activated by the sound of the dog barking should not be used. It is likely to confuse and disorient your dog, rather than resolve the problem. If there is no improvement in the dog's behavior, discuss the problem with your veterinarian.

Even if you have a mixed-breed dog you should be able to take part in competitions at certain shows. Dog periodicals list forthcoming shows and breed societies also provide information on events that may be of particular interest to you. Entering your dog at a top dog show can be a

10
Showing

very satisfying experience, but considerable dedication is needed and the financial rewards are almost nonexistent in most cases. You will probably need to set up kennels as well, which involves much greater committment than owning a single family pet. You will need a keen eye to assess your puppies at an early age so that you do not let a potential top dog slip through your grasp. It is important to be familiar with the show standard requirements for the breed, but this is no substitute for being able to appreciate the actual qualities of the breed.

why show your dog?

How to show your dog to the best advantage—and enjoy the occasion.

WHAT CAN I DO TO INCREASE THE LIKELIHOOD OF WINNING?

- If it has all the innate traits of a winner, train your dog. The best specimen won't win its class in a show if it isn't properly trained.
- Have your dog "faulted" by a member of your club. Be sure of your grooming. Don't over-groom or use the wrong type of brushes or combs on your dog's coat.
- Take classes in showmanship that are sponsored by your club. Dress properly, and learn to exhibit your dog in such a way that it is presented to the best advantage. Relax. Dog shows are fun. Don't be deterred just because you don't win the first time.
- After your class has shown, if your dog was not placed, ask the judge to tell you what you or your dog did wrong.

HOW WILL I KNOW IF MY PUPPY IS A FUTURE CHAMPION?

- Have it evaluated by a friend who is showing the same breed. Study the breed conformation standard and see how your dog compares.
- Write to the AKC for information about rules and regulations of dog shows. Join an all-breed dog club or better yet, a specialty club for your breed, and enter your dog in their "puppy matches," which are basically the same as shows, only less formal.
- Write to the AKC at 5580 Centerview Drive, Suite 200, Raleigh, NC 27606-3390, or call (919) 233-3600.

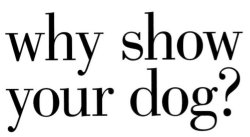

WHAT MAKES A CHAMPION DOG?

- This varies according to the country in which you are showing.
- In the United States, a dog must accumulate at least 15 championship points, which include two major wins.
- A "major" win is one that has sufficient class competition to earn the dog at least three points. It must record at least three separate wins under three different judges.
- After a dog has successfully reached this status, a prefix "Ch" is added to its name.

HOW MUCH TRAINING WILL MY DOG REQUIRE?

- Your dog must be able to respond to the basic commands, and especially to walk on a leash without pulling ahead or dragging behind.
- One of the greatest challenges when you first show a young dog is that it can be distracted by its fellow competitors.
- An experienced show dog will have learned to ignore them.

WHAT TYPE OF SHOW SHOULD I ENTER?

- At first, enter your puppy in fun matches that are sponsored by all-breed and specialty clubs.
- When you and your class instructors believe that you and your dog are doing well enough, try your hand in an open show.
- The obedience ring is another avenue of showing that may appeal to you. Special classes are offered by clubs in both conformation and obedience showing.

MY DOG IS A MIXED BREED, BUT A REAL CLOWN. CAN I SHOW HIM IN ANY EVENTS?

- In order to enter AKC shows and compete for points, ribbons, and rosettes, your dog must be a purebred and registered with that association.
- These AKC-sanctioned events include conformation shows, obedience trials, field trials, agility trials, herding trials, and others.
- There are, however, some city- or county-sponsored events that are great fun to participate in. These usually take place at fairs or special days and include parades, dress-up classes, cart pulling, Frisbee contests, and the like.
- There are also other organizations, such as United States Dog Agility Association, that open their competitions to purebred and mixed breed alike.

preparation & procedure

Getting your dog ready for a show and being aware of what to expect when you get there.

HOW DOES THE JUDGE SELECT THE WINNER?

- The judge assesses each entrant against the breed conformation standard.
- He or she observes how the dog moves and behaves, as the handler walks it around the show ring, and also examines the dog closely to check its soundness and condition.

HOW SHOULD I PREPARE MY DOG AND MYSELF FOR THE EVENT, BEFORE ENTERING THE SHOW RING?

HOW DO THE DIFFERENT GROUP SYSTEMS OPERATE?

- The various breeds are divided into groups, typically on the basis of their function. There are significant differences in categorizations, however, from one country to another. In Britain, for example, the Kennel Club (KC) divides the recognized breeds into six basic categories: hounds, gundogs, working dogs, toy dogs, terriers, and a utility group.
- The AKC has seven groups: Hound, Sporting, Terriers, Working, Herding, Non-Sporting, and Toy. But direct comparisons are impossible, because the actual categorization of the individual breeds also varies.
- Not all the breeds officially recognized by the AKC are accepted by the KC. Moreover, the listings are subject to change as new breeds gain acceptance. Obtain current listings from the AKC or the national kennel club of the relevant country.

HOW SHOULD I PREPARE BEFORE THE SHOW?

- Groom your dog to conform perfectly to its breed standard. A bath and simple grooming should be sufficient for short-coated dogs, but in other cases, you may want the help of an experienced groomer.
- Check the schedule carefully to be certain that your dog is entered in the correct class.
- A mistake would mean disqualification.

- Plan ahead as much as possible. Dress to complement your dog's appearance, and have your show entry number clearly pinned. Encourage your dog to relieve itself beforehand.
- Don't offer a drink while waiting that could wet its coat.
- Check your dog's grooming just before you enter the ring and don't fuss over your dog as the judge approaches.

index

acknowledgments

Quarto would like to acknowledge and thank the following for pictures used inside this book:

Norvia Behling: 157;
Marc Henri: 100 tl, 107 b;
Sally Anne Thompson: 155 tr;
Jane Burton/Warren Photography: title page, 24 r, 27, 29 l, 32, 33 r, 34, 35, 36, 37 t, 38, 41 t, 42, 45, 46 tl, 47, 49 br, 50 b, 55 r, 56 l, 60, 63, 65, 68 l & r, 69 l, 70, 71 t & b, 73 b, 74 l, 78 r, 79 t, 80 t & b, 81 t, 82 tl, tr & br, 83, 96, 99, 100 r, 102 l, 111, 112 b, 113, 114, 116, 118, 120, 122, 124 t & b, 125, 127 t & b, 128 t, 132 t & b, 134 b, 135 b, 138 tr, 142 149 b,150, 153.

All other photographs are the copyright of Quarto Publishing plc.
With help from Nicky.